Y - BOOKS DRAMA

TWO PLAYS

FINGERS ONLY

Originally known as "Lagos, Yes Lagos"

———— AND ————

A MAN NAMED MOKAI

ADE-YEMI AJIBADE

Y-Books
(a division of Associated Book-Makers Nigeria Limited)

Published by

Y–Books
(a division of Associated Book-Makers Nigeria Limited)
18 Adefioye Crescent
Off State Hospital Road, Ring Road
P.M.B 5561
Ibadan, Nigeria

Area Offices and Branches

Ibadan • Lagos • Jos • Kano • Abeokuta
Port-Harcourt • Benin

© Yemi Ajibade, 2001
   First published, 2001

ISBN 978-2659-88-6

Printed in Nigeria by

Fingers Only

(Originally "Lagos , Yes Lagos")

DEDICATION

To my parents:
Ajibade Adepoju Akande Omo Oladimeji
Wuraola Salamotu Rebecca Amoke (nee Al'kadri)

THE PLAY

About the Play

Baba Osa, the local master pick-pocket, has a guest comrade-in-arms from the city —*Josiah*. Together with *Mugun Yaro, Baba Osa's* apprentice, they team up for action. It all starts in *Baba Osa's* den: on to the bustling market place, and then back to the den. All in the course of a day.

Place: A small railway market town some thirty kilometres north-west of Lagos Island (not Ikeja).

Time: A time when Europe was on fire: Germany was roving round the continent, subjugating one nation after the other. Britain was combing African villages in her colonies for people, putting them in uniforms — to help her win the war against the Axis: Germany and her allies. The vibration of the Second World War has reached this small town.

Premiered by the Black Theatre Co-operative of Britain, at The Factory Theatre, London; moved to Battersea Arts Centre; and Albany Empire—Directed by Mustapha Matura — *all in 1982.*

CHARACTERS

Mugun Yaro:	Eleven-year-old apprentice to Baba Osa. — **Chris Tummings**
Baba Osa:	Master pick-pocket. — **Christopher Asante**
Josiah:	Another pick-pocket on a non-professional visit to Baba Osa. — **T-Bone Wilson**
Mama Taiye:	Local Market woman. — **Shope Shodeinde**
Taiye:	College girl: daughter of Mama Taiye. — **Judith Jacob**
Mama Adisa:	Perfume-seller from the city. — **Ena Cabayo**
Awanatu:	Girl-friend to Baba Osa — **Judith Jacob**
Corporal Layi:	Local police officer. — **Raymond Page**
Sergeant Momo:	New officer in charge. — **Malcom Frederick**

ACT I

*Three cocks crow; one after the other. Lights go up on stage. Simultaneously a boy rises groggily from his mat on the floor. There is a long settee and a chair on stage. The boy hurries to an exit that serves as an entrance to another room, from which we hear heavy snoring. He hesitates, and then peers through. The boy is known as **Mugun Yaro**. **Baba Osa** is snoring away in the very near room. As **Mugun** opens the door, the snoring becomes heavier.*

Mugun Yaro:	Wake up master! The cock has crowed.
Baba Osa:	Hum... aaa... go away... *(He goes back to sleep. He begins to snore again)*
Mugun Yaro:	Master, the cock has crowed; wake up master!!
Baba Osa:	*(Enters; wrapped to the waist in white sheet)* Hum... What? The cock! eh eh! *(He stretches and yawns)* Ah good lad. *(He's using his chewing stick)*
Mugun Yaro:	The cock has just crowed.
Baba Osa:	*(Looks around)* Ok... I heard you. Where is Josiah? Where is he?
Mugun Yaro:	I don't know sir. I just woke up myself.
Baba Osa:	Never mind. Maybe he's gone to ease himself in the bush. But I warned him not to go out in this town after dark, well!. Mugun Yaro, you go and get water ready for me to bathe.
Mugun Yaro:	I discovered too late last night that the water nearly finished in the jar.

5

Baba Osa:	Why? You mean there is no water for me to bathe with... and you and I slept under the same roof? Your block head to the dogs, you swine! Come closer!
Mugun Yaro:	Sorry sir. It will never happen again. I was too busy roasting the chickens for supper last night. I beg sir!
Baba Osa:	Come closer I say. *(He hits him)*
Mugun Yaro:	Yea! Yea! *(Wails and screams in agony as he tumbles and rolls on the floor crashing against the chairs).*
Baba Osa:	Shut up! You son of a coward. How many times have I warned you not to make that horrible noise when I hit you? *(He hits again).*
Mugun Yaro:	I have stopped sir! *(Trying to suppress his pain).*
Baba Osa:	You! *(As he delivers four more thudding blows, Mugun Yaro grunts heavily as each lands).* That's right now. Never forget your discipline!
Mugun Yaro:	No sir. I will never forget it.
Baba Osa:	Go immediately to catch one of those early water hawkers. Away before I smash your wooden skull.
Mugun Yaro:	Yes sir! *(He turns to go, crashes into Josiah who is entering doorway).* Sorry Junior master!
Josiah:	*(Dressed in casual native clothes — long **dashiki**, trousers and sandals with **Bourdillon Felt Hat**)* Eh Mugun, what's the matter? *(Mugun escapes. shutting the door behind him).* Baba Osa, what's happening to him?
Baba Osa:	Everything is ok, just a bit of timely correction. Where have you been so early in

6

	the morning, Josiah?
Josiah:	Just took a stroll around in the neighbourhood, to think things out...
Baba Osa:	Listen, and listen carefully. You are my guest. I know this town, and I warn you to keep off the streets at all dark hours. Please don't do it again. If even you want to ease yourself, do it in the bathroom and Mugun Yaro will dispose of it in the afternoon.
Josiah:	I am sorry.
Baba Osa:	Later on, I will tell you the reason and you'll understand my anxiety.
Josiah:	OK Baba Osa. *(Pause)* You know, I haven't had a chance to talk to you alone since I arrived last night.
Baba Osa:	Plenty of time, Josie.
Josiah:	This is important. *(Pause)* I ought to let you know... that I am on the run.
Baba Osa:	*(Shocked; then laughs)* The police again?
Josiah:	No, it's the Army... They are after me.
Baba Osa:	*(Ponders seriously)* You enlisted?
Josiah:	I didn't. Just a week ago, on the eve of my discharge from prison, the Governor asked me down to his office...
Baba Osa:	I didn't even know you were doing time.
Josiah:	Just a short spell. First he said I was a well-known top operator in the city. I was proud to hear that in a way. Then he asked if I'd like to use my experience to help the Empire win the war. I said it'll be a joy; but I had to think it over.
	After my release the next morning, I was hustled into a waiting army lorry at the prison gate. The two military police wouldn't

7

utter a word. But the other civilians in the lorry — all senior boys from King's College — were chatting nervously about going straight overseas into the battle front. I really don't mind helping the Empire out. But I thought it was a cheek to grab me like I was a stray chicken. My mind was ticking over as the lorry moved on. My old lady far away in the village; you: then our colleagues that went overseas, and were never heard of. You know Obeche, Saibu, Laisi Togo...

Baba Osa: *(Interrupts him)* With the 81st West African Division, wasn't it?

Josiah: *(Nods)* The lorry was on **Moloney Bridge** when I cut loose. In a flash I was wallowing in the lagoon. There was noise everywhere as I disappeared into the swamp up the creek. I lay low at Idimu village until yesterday...

Baba Osa: That's it?... *(Josiah nods ,Baba Osa nods and shakes his head. and smiles)* Josie the cat! Josie no dey trouble trouble; na trouble dey trouble Josie...

Josiah: *(Forces a smile)* It is a serious matter, Baba Osa.

Baba Osa: I know. But they won't be looking for you. Ever!

Josiah: They are always raiding houses for deserters everywhere in the city. And when they are caught..!

Baba Osa: You didn't take their uniforms, did you?

Josiah: Me? I didn't even get near their barracks.

Baba Osa: *(Emphatically)* That's what their white officers care most about. Uniforms! Always saluting it, no matter where or when... Run

	away; but leave their uniforms alone; and they won't be bothered. After all, lots of our people are still joining up everyday... *(Confidentially)* Only when some of them find they can't stand it that they make for the bush, with all the uniforms; boots, haversack and all. That's what gets the army.
Josiah:	But what on earth would anyone do with the uniforms?
Baba Osa:	*(Shrugs)* They tear away the fancy badges and flog them to farm labourers... Wait! *(He looks left and right; disappears upstage and reappears with an army sweater)*... See; thick and hardwearing. I use it under my garment during harmattan season.
Josiah:	*(Impressed)* Baba Osa! You borrowed it!
Baba Osa:	*(Admiring the sweater)* Hard cash... Never put borrowed things on my skin... *(Josiah feels it)* That's what they go after the deserters for.
Josiah:	*(Chuckles)* Funny there were times I had thought of signing on of my own free will, you know....With the proper send-off parties like the other boys of our profession.
Baba Osa:	Me too. The first time I saw the new recruits doing the European war-dance my blood boiled in my veins. I longed to be there right in the hot front somewhere, performing heroics you know; gunning down the enemy by the dozens to help the Empire out.
Josiah:	I felt the same, the very first time too.
Baba Osa:	But then this tall European officer stepped forward to announce that recruits would be earning £2 per month *(Adds with contempt)*

9

	plus free bowls of soup and gari! Me? £2 for thirty days!'
Josiah:	That's the standard wages for the gunners.
Baba Osa:	Some of the villagers were joining up on the spot. I just let Mugun Yaro loose on the Officer; and the kid came back with a nice looking instrument from his haversack. I'll show it to you. *(Josiah manages a chuckle)* A lousy £2 a month for a bullet in the gullet!
Josiah:	People don't look at it that way, when they join.
Baba Osa:	I do. It's a question of appreciation, Josie. I come from a long line of warriors — the real professionals as you may know. No cowardice in my vein — only prudence. That's why I'm glad you melted. *(Josiah brightens up a bit)* What difference will it make to us who wins... Hitler, English; America or any other son-of-a-bitch you care to mention. *(Pause as Josiah thinks)* On Market days here, you can hear the old villagers chatting away about how the Europeans helped stop the wars among the tribes here. Now, for one reason or another, they start a big one among themselves, and they want us to help out...
Josiah:	*(Interrupts with superior knowledge)* Not like that...
Baba Osa:	*(Brushes Josiah's remark aside and continues)* Alright. War is made for the braves... But for what?... £2 a month with stew and gari... And then what?
Josiah:	*(Educating him)* No. No. You've got it wrong, Baba Osa. This one is for the Empire... Everyone!
Baba Osa:	*(Sarcastically)* Yes? In that case, I've got my own empire here to look after.

10

	(Confidentially) **It's the whiteman's war, Josie...** Let them fight it out, and then we can **take on whatever master comes along.** *(Joking)* **If you ask me, right now, I am yearning for a change of Governor here: be him German, or Spanish like er... er... er...** Santa Isabel in Fernando Po. *(They both laugh).*
Josiah:	You're never serious —you old son-of-a-gun!
Baba Osa:	Every problem has its solution... *(Judiciously)* Ignore it! And if the problem is bold enough, let it reappear. In time, it comes up with its own solution. *(They laugh)* We are behind time, Josie. *(Josiah nods)* Do retire to the verandah while I do my supplication.
Josiah:	Yes, of course... *(He exits)*
Baba Osa:	*(Kneels and touches the floor and his forehead in turn. In solemn and deliberate sing-song he continues)*

Earth! Earth!! Earth!!!
(He shakes some object that produces sound like a giant box full of watches each time he says 'earth')

I call you.
Do not call me back in a hurry.
Keep me and feed me.
That I may not die young;
That I may not grow old into poverty.
Earth! You are the mother of the market.
Sons trample on you arrogantly, slaves
Match on your surface rudely.
They bring their wares from far and
Beyond and barter on your still surface.

You never complain.
Yet when they leave for their villages, they
Leave nothing for you, but unsaleable rubbish.
You can be kind; you can be cruel.
You first feed children of man!

You then feed on man and his children.

(He shakes again violently as if possessed)

Be with me today.
Whatever I do in the market today, I do
Witches of the market are my mothers.
Wizards of the market are my fathers.
Albinos never see properly in daylight.
May people never see me properly.
During all our operations today.
So be it. *(Three times)*

Josiah:	*(He knocks)* Is It alright to come in now? Mugun Yaro is back with water...
Baba Osa:	Come right in, Josiah. *(Enters Josiah)* We must get ready immediately. I can see it is broad daylight now. I have a great feeling it is going to be a prosperous market. *(He shouts suddenly)* Mugun Yaro!
Mugun Yaro:	*(Peeps and withdraws)* Sir, the water is ready for you sir.
Baba Osa:	*(Shaking his head)* That boy can be fantastic after he's had his dose. He is like a race horse ... always needing whipping for top performance. *(Jokingly)* What's the matter, Josiah?
Josiah:	I'm ok... I just wonder about life, sometimes.
Baba Osa:	Don't wonder about it. Live. That's my style to it. If you want some hot pap and bean cake, Mugun Yaro will see to it. I always leave some money on him as petty-cash. *(He shouts)* Mugun Yaro!

12

Mugun Yaro:	*(Rushes in)* Sir!
Baba Osa:	Josiah will tell you what he wants. And fill your own belly too if you must. I don't want anything. I've got to earn my meal, otherwise I feel guilty. *(Laughs)* Take no notice, Josie! *(Hums a light cheerful African tune)*
Mugun Yaro:	Junior master, how much pap and bean cake would you like sir?
Josiah:	No, I don't want anything to eat either. Just get me two sticks of cigarette. Bandmaster or Guinea Gold brand.
Mugun Yaro:	Yes sir. *(He goes)*
Baba Osa:	I didn't want to say much in front of Mugun Yaro... See... this is a nice little town. Exciting. We are surrounded by several villages, but for the odd stray soldiers, we wouldn't even know that there is a World War going on. Prosperity is here, Josie... But there is the other side... tough, violent, grim... unspeakable really... Men of our profession disapear without trace from time to time in this town. The night guards consist of professional hunters who render their service to the community without pay. To them a suspected thief is only good for target shooting. The bullet is for real. No corpse; no exhibit, no story.
Josiah:	Just like that...
Baba Osa:	But it doesn't deter the die-hard night operators though. Professional hazards they call it... I'm a daylight man... a job for the police. But the hunters know me. They also know that I know how badly they wish to meet me, in a dark alley some night — even on an innocent stroll.

13

Josiah:	And you still hang around?
Baba Osa:	Why not? I've got a little kingdom carved for myself here. We have a police force of three, with a sergeant as the top man — and I am the major. *(They both laugh)* The rule of the game!
Josiah:	*(Good-heartedly)* ...the human mercury!
Baba Osa:	That's me, Josie... *(Goes to bathe as Mugun Yaro enters)*
Mugun Yaro:	Here, Junior master. A whole tinful of Bandmaster cigarette. *(Proudly)* An unopened one too, sir.
Josiah:	A whole tin of fifty! I said two sticks of cigarette!
Mugun Yaro:	I heard you sir, but it is easier to get a whole tin than to get two sticks sir. *(Smiling)* And they both cost the same price.
Josiah:	*(Laughs quietly realizing what Mugun Yaro means)* You are a smart kid, Mugun Yaro.
Mugun Yaro:	You haven't seen anything sir, I mean real operation.
Josiah:	Is Mugun Yaro your real name? You don't sound Hausa to me.
Mugun Yaro:	Some Hausa friends of my master gave me the nickname. Master said that it was because I am very small and that nobody ever suspects anything while I borrow things from them. I'm not Hausa. In fact, my village is only about ten miles away from here.
Josiah:	What is the meaning of Mugun?
Mugun Yaro:	I don't know either, but I like it. Are you going to stay with us for sometime, sir? I mean I will like it very much if you do.

14

Josiah:	I don't know yet. Why will you like it if I stay on?
Mugun Yaro:	Because my big master said that you are very powerful... that you have plenty of magical power, with which you could "borrow" loot from a whole lorry. That will be very exciting... I think.
Josiah:	He told you that, did he?
Mugun Yaro:	Please sir, don't tell him that I say anything about it or I'll get much beating.
Josiah:	No, I won't. How old are you, Mugun?
Mugun Yaro:	Next Christmas will be my twelfth. I was born on Christmas eve, so my mother said. That's why my real name is Abiodun.
Josiah:	I see. Then you'll be twelve next Christmas?
Mugun Yaro:	Yes sir. Master said you use to operate in the city?
Josiah:	Yes.
Mugun Yaro:	They say the sea is so large that no one can see the end of it. And that the ships that travel on it to Europe are larger and more populous than a whole city? *(Baba Osa is approaching quickly)* Master is coming.
Baba Osa:	*(Humming as he comes. He has changed into a big embroidered agbada garment, trousers, clothen cap and sandals to match. With great alacrity)* Mugun Yaro!
Mugun Yaro:	*(Stands alert)* Yes sir!
Baba Osa:	Mugun Yaro! Yaro!!
Mugun Yaro:	Great respect sir!
Baba Osa:	I have a dream!
Mugun Yaro:	You wear a crown laced with jewels.
Baba Osa:	I have a dream!

15

Mugun Yaro:	You wear a regal robe!
Baba Osa:	I have a dream!
Mugun Yaro:	You walk with a staff of coral beads!
Baba Osa:	And what?
Mugun Yaro:	Your children shall bury you with great honour and pomp!
Baba Osa:	(Bursts into laughter, Josiah and Mugun join in) That's right Mugun. Now sing your song for Josiah.
Mugun Yaro:	*(Does some weird steps and sings)* Mba ambamba Kimba. Mba ambamba Kimba. Sakata da doya ba. Kojere ba Mugun Yaro ba o!
Josiah:	What's all these strange things you are both saying?
Baba Osa:	They are just passwords — mainly to train Mugun Yáro's memory. Now we go down to work. The market must be nearly full now.
	(He produces an old binoculars from under the settee. Josiah looks curious) A fantastic instrument. The one Mugun borrowed from the European officer... *(He dusts the binoculars. He tries it in turn with Josiah)* Got your tools Mugun Yaro?
Mugun Yaro:	Yes sir.
Baba Osa:	We are going to do the three in one. Mugun works; you chat, I observe. After operation, we split and meet back here, ok?
Josiah:	Ok. What if anything goes wrong?
Baba Osa:	I'll take care of that. You just pretend you've never seen Mugun Yaro before. *(To Mugun)* Mugun Yaro keep your nerves, I'll look after you, ok?
Mugun Yaro:	Alright sir!

16

MARKET SCENE

*(Lights up and we hear the general market noise rumbles in the background. A **backdrop with painted African village** market scene is suggested here. Baba Osa is perched elevated to the ceiling in a remote upstage corner. A woman, Mama Taiye, and her daughter, Taiye, are setting up their wares: pots, pans clothing for the market. Mama Taiye is simply dressed in long head ties, short roomy buba (blouse) and a wide wrapper in tie-dye. She is barefooted. Taiye wears a play frock of school uniform type. She dons a beret with school badge and sandals. Baba Osa is busy viewing with his binoculars in offstage directions. He directs, points and waves his instructions energetically.*

Sometimes coolly, sometimes excitedly. Mugun runs in from opposite direction. He scuttles: looks at Baba Osa and backs up. He moves sideways and then carefully forward on tiptoe. He is like a marionette. All his attention is focussed alternatively on Baba Osa and on the yet invisible victim. He exits finally DR.(We hear a female voice hawking from off stage. "Fine Perfume! Fine Fine Lavender. Fine Fine Lavender. Roses of Arabia! Pines of Europe! Turari of Africa undiluted... come one, come all".)

Josiah enters UR, takes a momentary look at Baba Osa, freezes and then exits DL in a flash.(Mama Adisa, the hawker, enters DR.) Baba Osa turns away. She stops as she recognises Taiye and her mother. Both had been oblivious of the movements around them.

Mama Adisa enters, carrying her wares. Several small and large bottles of perfume and pieces of lavender wood and incense. She shouts from a distance).

Mama Adisa:	Good morning o, Mama Taiye. *(Across their wares 15 yards apart)* How do you do?
Mama Taiye:	I'm alright. How is the family?
Mama Adisa:	Thank God everyone is well. I see Taiye comes with you. Is she on holidays already?
Mama Taiye:	Well... sort of. *(To Taiye confidentially)* Open your mouth and say hello. You school girls

17

	are so dumb. You lack culture and native manners. God knows what they teach you in these schools of yours.
Taiye:	I just didn't want to interrupt your greetings. I might be accused of being forward or rude.
Mama Taiye:	Never mind that. You always have answers ready for everything. Are you going to go across to Mama Adisa and say hello or stand there explaining things?
Mama Adisa:	Leave Taiye alone. The children of today are not like us, you must understand. It requires a lot of patience to deal with them. Adisa is no different. *(Directed to Taiye)* My dear, how are you?
Taiye:	*(Approaching)* I am alright, thank you, ma. Please forgive me, ma, I didn't mean to ignore you. .
Mama Adisa:	Never mind, never mind. My prayer is that may God preserve the lives of you young ones and help you in your learning.
Taiye:	Amen.
Mama Adisa:	Here, to buy anything you like *(Coins exchange hands)*
Taiye:	Thank you, ma.
Mama Adisa:	So you are on holiday already, that is rather early I think.
Taiye:	Not exactly, ma. It is an enforced holiday. Our college and the boys college are being moved into the country. And the premises are to be taken over by the army. How is Adisa, ma? Hope you hear from him regularly?
Mama Adisa:	My dear, you mean you haven't heard?

Taiye:	Heard what? I've heard nothing, ma.
Mama Adisa:	Adisa has exposed me to the ridicule of the entire neighbourhood. He took off from his uncle in Lagos, pretending to spend the weekend here. That was fourteen days ago today. We have not heard from him since.
Taiye:	*(Shocked)* Baba O! That's very serious!
Mama Adisa:	That's what I'm in, Taiye. I've been to three medicine men. They all say they could see him in the company of elderly people, marching up and down. The great Ifa Priest across the river said he could see him trying to join the army.
Taiye:	But couldn't that be wrong, ma? Adisa is too young to join the army.
Mama Adisa:	I hear that Europeans don't mind kid soldiers; especially now that all sorts have joined in. And that priest! He is famous throughout the district for his clairvoyance. Anyway I am leaving for the city tonight. I'll have to comb the soldiers barracks to bring my boy back. *(Pause)* Better go help your mother, I'll see you later.
Taiye:	Alright, ma. But try to cheer up. Adisa will turn up somehow by the power of God.
Mama Adisa:	Amen, my dear, God will look after you all. *(She exits UR)*
Mama Taiye:	*(To Taiye)* She's been telling you about Adisa.
Taiye:	Yes. Very sad...
	(Enters Mugun on tiptoe DR and moves UR and freezes. Josiah enters DL and exchanges a strong glance with Mama Taiye and exits DR as Baba Osa directs)
Mama Taiye:	*(In low voice)* Sh! Sh!! Here he comes; please don't look.

19

Taiye:	*(Looks at Mugun)* Who?
Mama Taiye:	The nameless one. That's the rat that feeds in full view of the householder. Light as a feather. I think he spots a victim nearby.
Taiye:	That small boy?
Mama Taiye:	Small boy! I've seen him steal a sewing machine with heavy iron stand, while everyone but the owner was looking. His master is not around yet. Keep your eyes open, and you may see something you've never seen before today.
Taiye:	Thieves?
Mama Taiye:	Shut up! Looks like that tall man is with the boy today, but he's a stranger. He too must be one *(Pause)* ...God knows who they're after.
Taiye:	Shall I go for the police then?
Mama Taiye:	*(Nudges her)* Sh! Sh! Shut up!
	(Baba Osa directs, Mugun rises eagerly. Mama Adisa's voice approaches. Josiah backs up on Stage DR. Hides. Enters Mama Adisa. Mugun and Josiah converge on her)
Josiah:	Have you Saserabia perfume?
Mama Adisa:	Yes, by the dozen. I also have Tutan, Jebe, Francais, Jaman, all kinds of perfume in fact. And they are the cheapest in the whole market. Here, the Saserabia pure undiluted — smell.
	(Opens one for Josiah who sniffs it. Mugun feels the woman around her bottom. He stops on something and works on it until the end of the scene)
Josiah:	*(Sniffs)* Uh... un... very very good. This is exactly what I want. How much for one?

20

Mama Adisa:	I sell them for 25 shillings each, but since it is you, well, my firstborn is a boy, I leave it for you for 20 shillings.
Josiah:	Fifteen shillings.
Mama Adisa:	Please don't be like that. You men never know how to price things. You cut five shillings off just like that eh... well take it, as a special concession to you, because you are my first customer this morning. I'll wrap it for you. *(She makes a move to wrap it)*
Josiah:	Not yet! I can only pay thirteen shillings.
Mama Adisa:	What's this? I didn't get them from smugglers you know. Don't you want me to eat something myself?
Josiah:	I want everybody to eat a little.
Mama Adisa:	Put a shilling more and take it at fourteen shillings and that's selling at cost price.
Josiah:	I really can't put a shilling more.
Mama Adisa:	*(Unduly familiar)* Eh listen, handsome young man! I can guess what you want it for. You want to prepare love charm with it, so you can charm any woman you desire. O yes, don't I know? *(Giggles)* Well, I tell you it is more potent than anything I know. But, in buying the ingredients for love charm, one must not be too tight-fisted. In the long run, women can't stand tight-fisted men you know. *(She laughs phonily)* Well, I bless you my man, God bless you and whatsoever you are using it for. Take it for thirteen shillings but don't spread the news.

(Mugun is busy interferring with the woman. He is cutting some bundle off her with a knife. Holding the knife with his teeth; he takes out the scissors to do the job. Josiah tests the perfume all through).

21

Josiah:	Thank you. But I want more than one. I am a petty trader from far away village myself.
Mama Adisa:	Don't give me that. You look every inch a dashing young man from some city... Lagos I might say.
Josiah:	*(Laughs)* Not all villagers carry the emblem. *(Mugun finishes and exits UR fast)*
Mama Adisa:	Of course not. I'm only joking. Well pick as many as you want and I'll make the addition.
Josiah:	I'll want two dozen. But it will have to be at the rate of ten shillings each. I will pay now if that's agreed.
Mama Adisa:	I can't catch that very well. Do you come here to buy perfume or you are just wondering about the market? Ten shillings he says! You realise that you are the first one to deal with me today... um? That this might set the pattern of sales for me the whole day? Please don't spoil my day. May the spirit of wealth abide with you... Take it at twelve shillings. I will be able to sell only a dozen to you, because it is clearly at a loss.
Josiah:	No, I can't. You don't want to do business with me. I must go. I have other things to buy. *(Strolls away casually)*
Mama Adisa:	Go? Go where? You call yourself a trader, and you behave like the firstborn of poverty itself. Early in the morning! You wretch; with neck like that of a giraffe; your knees knocking at vertically opposite angles... You never intended to buy anything in the first place... you bastard; eyes like an owl's and back view like that of a camel.
	Profits and prosperity shall never come your way. *(Pause)* Oh my Creator, what have I done to deserve this? I performed all the

rites before leaving home. I hope this trend of evil influence will not continue today. God, my conscience is clean as the spring water. *(She rearranges her bottles and starts hawking)* Lavender, perfume... laven...

(She stops to feel her clothing. Quickly she puts down her merchandise and feels her clothing frantically round her waist). What's this..! *(She undoes her outer wrapper, revealing* **yeri** *— short African shirt — beneath a short blouse showing her midriff)* Where is it...? *(She is shaking and thoroughly confused. She drops her wrapper on the floor almost unconsciously)* My money bag... am I dreaming or what?

(She finally produces a clothen belt from under her skirt) ...It's cut! ...When? Must have been at the butchers... no... maybe on the lorry... Where? *(Baba Osa discreetly throws his weighted hook on the wrapper and pulls it fast to himself and exits with the wrapper)*

(She shouts)...O! people of the market, I'm bedevilled! I'm finished! I'm lost! My money... *(She cries)* All gone... Hurricane's struck at my homestead. *(She discovers her wrapper has gone as well. Looks about her)* My wrapper... Where's my wrapper... my money... What's happening? *(She's now terrified as well)* What's this? Police! Police!

Taiye: Mother! You see what happened. We could have prevented it.

Mama Taiye: Shut up, I say. It is not our business. One doesn't protect others' heads while the eagle snatches one's own away.

Taiye: Mother, but it could happen to you too.

23

Mama Taiye:	It will happen to me, if you keep on. Well, I will tell you something. I live here: and those pickpockets can sort me out. They are most dangerous and mean, when seeking revenge against anyone who interferes with their business. The former bicycle repairer from Arigbajo tried to tackle them. One by one his bicycles disappeared. They then raided his home, taking everything including brooms and his baby's nappies! He too has since disappeared, leaving his young wife and child in the care of his relatives. Is that what you want for me, Taiye? *(Pauses for answer)* Answer me!
Taiye:	But they needn't know who reports them to the police.
Mama Taiye:	They'll find out sooner than later. Besides, I'm sure the tall one who pretends to bargain knew we saw everything. Oh they are as clever as they are evil.
Taiye:	Still, someone has to stop them.
Mama Taiye:	That person won't be you, my girl. Now talk about something else or shut up!
	(We hear Police whistle, footsteps and Mama Adisa wailing, from offstage. She rushes in followed by a Police Corporal)
Mama Adisa:	*(Stops, indicating the spot where she was before)* Here... I was here... I'm sure.
	(The Policeman moves aggressively, inquiring;towards Taiye and her mother. Mama Taiye throws up her hands and shakes her head before the Policeman could say a word)

BLACK OUT

END OF ACT I

24

ACT II

(Back at Baba Osa's Den. Baba Osa is humming to himself)

〰〰〰〰〰〰〰〰〰〰〰〰〰〰〰〰〰〰〰〰〰〰〰〰〰〰〰〰〰

Mugun Yaro:	*(Breathlessly runs in)* Master! I did it, master. I did it. Here... *(Handing over the bag full of money)*
Baba Osa:	Relax and stop beaming like an idiot. I saw everything. I watched it all happen just as I planned it. But you nearly goofed it, you clumsy son of a goat. *(In unfriendly tone)* Come here! Give me your left ear.
Mugun Yaro:	Please master, what have I done wrong? I did everything as I was told throughout the operation.
Baba Osa:	Not quite. *(Grips Mugun by the ear and twists it. Mugun groans in pain)*
Mugun Yaro:	My ear! ...Ooh... it hurts.
Baba Osa:	How many times have I told you never to dip your whole hand in people's pockets? Did I not tell you always to use fingers and fingers only?
Mugun Yaro:	*(Groaning as Baba Osa squeezes harder)* You did, sir.
Baba Osa:	Then why did you disobey me? I saw your whole arm buried in the woman's skirt or didn't I? *(He squeezes harder)*
Mugun Yaro:	Yes master, but the bag was tied way up to her waist. I had to lift her outer wrapper to get it. I'm sorry, master.
Baba Osa:	*(Throws Mugun free)* You very nearly bungled the whole thing — a perfect set-up

	like that with nothing for you to worry about. ...Now correct yourself?
	(He turns his back on Mugun and moves about casually. Mugun follows him trying to take something from his master's pocket. Eventually Mugun steadily lifts a handkerchief from his master with two fingers aloft. Baba Osa turns to him satisfied) Now what's wrong with that, eh?
Mugun Yaro:	Nothing sir.
Baba Osa:	Now where is Josiah? He ought to have been here now.
Mugun Yaro:	I left him still bargaining with the woman.
Baba Osa:	I saw him leave just before the woman began her Jeremiah wailing. I hope he is alright. *(Pause. Someone is approaching)* I think that's him coming.
Josiah:	*(Enters roaring with laughter)* This is one of the smoothest three-in-one operations I have been involved in for a long time.
Baba Osa:	That's our style here. But what kept you?
Josiah:	I took a long detour and got the way mixed up. I know everything was alright. *(Arrogantly)* No animal waylays the tiger!
Baba Osa:	*(Smiling)* Josie! Josie!! The torrent that clears all in its path!
Josiah:	*(Formally)* My homage to you, Baba Osa. Sea never dry.
Baba Osa:	Butterfly shall never fall over. *(They both laugh heartily)*
Josiah:	O! I'm beginning to feel hungry.
Baba Osa:	First things first. We must count the money now. Mugun Yaro, lock the door. Not that anyone dares show up here uninvited. But

26

	one mustn't tempt them. *(He unties the bag. It contains coins and notes)*
Josiah:	Oh there are currency notes in it as well.
Baba Osa:	Some of the papers are not money. *(He counts)* Seventeen pounds in notes. Now the coins. *(He begins to count without using words)* Give me a hand, Josiah.
Josiah:	With money, I don't mind at all. Remember, I said I'm starving.
Baba Osa:	My sweetheart will bring food in a minute.
Josiah:	I never like to eat food prepared by whores. I don't trust them.
Baba Osa:	This is not a whore. She is a respectably-married young lady. Real smooth and warm. You'll like her when she comes over. *(To Mugun)* Look at Mugun Yaro's eyes coming out of their sockets at the sight of money. *(All laugh)* Go prepare the goat in the yard ready for barbecue... And burn this. *(He hands over the clothen money bag to Mugun)*
Mugun Yaro:	Yes master. *(Cheerfully exits)*
Josiah:	Oh, I have missed the counting.
Baba Osa:	You can leave the rest, I'll count it. I can sing and count at the same time. *(Counts)* There you are. Five pounds, eight shillings in coins. That makes £22.8d altogether. Not bad eh?
Josiah:	I'll never guess that that poorly-dressed woman was that loaded.
Baba Osa:	I can smell them out no matter what their clothes. It is a matter of instinct based on experience in this part. *(Heavy sound of struggle and grunts of goat and Mugun Yaro is emanating from off stage)*
Josiah:	*(Alarmed)* What's going on out there?

Baba Osa:	That's Mugun Yaro and his cousin spelling it out. *(Loudly)* Kama shi Mugun Yaro! Kama shi!
Mugun Yaro:	Yes sir!
Baba Osa:	*(Bursts into laughter)* Here, hold on to this.
Josiah:	All eight pounds!
Baba Osa:	*(Takes a small wooden money box from under the chair, and pushes a pound note and some coins into it)* Mugun's private bank. I always put something aside for him after each operation.
Josiah:	... Very good idea...
Baba Osa:	Well, I'll keep the rest in reserve, hey!
	(More sound of struggle. This time accompanied by the splashes of water and Mugun Yaro's grunting)
Josiah:	Is he alright?
Baba Osa:	He is in control. That boy is a wizard when it comes to weird things. *(Goes to put his share away and comes back. He speaks throughout his short journey)* Sometime ago, we went to visit an Ibariba friend of mine — you'll meet him later. He prepared delicious barbecue with a borrowed goat which he'd drowned in a huge jar of water. The following day, I too borrowed a goat from the herds that stray around. But I nearly regretted it. The goat gave me a vicious kick on my forehead, narrowly missing my right eye. Thanks must be due to the protection charms I carry. Mugun was on the goat like a flash! We had our own barbecue that evening. Mugun saw to that. Since then we have been alternating chickens, guinea-fowls, and ducks with goats. He got this goat specially for you, when you arrived last night.

28

Josiah:	Barbecueing by drowning!
Baba Osa:	Yes. No bleating, no tell-tale blood around. Just the struggle and that, for Mugun Yaro, is a sport. *(Loudly abruptly)* Mugun Yaro!
Mugun Yaro:	*(Off stage)* Yes master! *(Enters)* I come sir.
Baba Osa:	How are you getting on with your cousin?
Mugun Yaro:	*(With enthusiasm)* It is already on the fire sir. *(Baba Osa and Josiah laugh)*
Baba Osa:	Go tell Awanatu that I want some food now — also that I have a guest. Here! *(He rushes to his room and reappears folding Mama Adisa's wrapper)* Tell her to dye it, immediately.
Mugun Yaro:	*(Puts it under his own garment)* Yes sir. *(Going)*
Baba Osa:	Take the short-cut across the yard.
Mugun Yaro:	Yes sir. *(Exits)*
Josiah:	But the boy appears clever.
Baba Osa:	That's the result of tough training. He was as dull and slow-witted as a lamb, when he first came here.
Josiah:	I still can't stop marvelling at the steadiness of his nerves when he was doing the operation on that woman.
Baba Osa:	Oh yes, he pulled it off alright. But, despite the fact that I have warned him always to use fingers only, he stuck his mosquito arm into the woman's arse. The woman did feel something, I'm sure; but was just too absorbed with your talking. Your contribution at that point was crucial.
Josiah:	But the so-called "Fingers Alone" theory can be a serious limitation and sometimes unpractical.

29

Baba Osa:	I don't think so, and neither did the old-timers. The good old Jaguda himself *(RIP)* was the first exponent of "fingers". Akin Devil, Sanni Wallet, Jo Big-spender, Obeche slow-motion lightning and several other top men of our profession are all finger-men. Tell me *one* who is not!
Josiah:	Baba Osa, nearly all the boys you've just mentioned talk in praise of "Fingers"; but they all perform according to situation. For instance, I've seen Akin Devil, the same gasser you just mentioned, give a virtuoso performance at Oyingbo market, in full view of everyone. Believe it or not, he disappeared right inside the huge garment of an Hausa cattle merchant to cut the poor man's bulging wallet. For good three minutes, there stood the merchant on what looked like four legs — chewing his cola-nut with ease. Akin did it — in his own way. Yet as you said, he always shouts "fingers only"!
Baba Osa:	Yes. You can always experiment and improvise, after you've become experienced; but the young ones I maintain, should be reared on "Fingers" system. It makes for discipline, and I want discipline for my boy.
Josiah:	Discipline... and what does it all add up to?
Baba Osa:	What exactly does that mean?
Josiah:	Well... *(Shrugs)* Nothing.
Baba Osa:	You're gloomy, Josie I don't like gloom.
Josiah:	I'm just being realistic, that's all.
Baba Osa:	About what?
Josiah:	One is entitled to reflect sometimes, don't you think?
Baba Osa:	On what?

Josiah:	On the past - our past.
Baba Osa:	Your past.
Josiah:	Alright; my past...
Baba Osa:	I've told you, I don't live in the past. I don't spend the whole of today thinking about my yesterdays. What's the use? I ran away from home; you ran away from home: the kid ran away from home... It's the same old story with nearly everyone in the profession...
Josiah:	Does it have to stay that way for ever?
Baba Osa:	It's life. I didn't start the kid on anything. Ask him. He came to the market, and refused to go back to his people. He was starving to death among gabbage when I found him. I did my best to send him back home but he wouldn't go. "Please master, don't send me back, master" he kept saying. What do I do eh?
Josiah:	I know you wouldn't start a kid on...
Baba Osa:	*(Defending)* I feed him; clothe him; teach him what I know. I protect him. *(Boastfully)* That boy can be caught borrowing the head-dress from any Chief in this town and nobody dare touch him. I make sure of that, and I stake my life on it.
Josiah:	I'm not thinking about the kid alone.
Baba Osa:	Then think about yourself and don't bring gloom to me. You hear! *(Pause)*
	(Josiah rises uncertainly)
Baba Osa:	Where are you going?
Josiah:	No where.
Baba Osa:	Sit down... *(Josiah doesn't move)* Josie! *(He sits)* You start the story. We are what we are. If Mugun is not here today, maybe he'd have

31

grown up in his village pinching **yams** and chickens from some poor farmer. Who knows? *(Shrugging)* And if he's not destined for the profession, time will look after that. *(Emphatically)* But while he is here, I'll make sure he doesn't miss out on discipline... *(Gloomily)* He'll take that away with him if nothing else *(Pause. Simply)* Mugun Yaro is an orphan. *(Josiah reacts with shock and sadness)*

Baba Osa: *(Warning)* He doesn't like talking about it though... Gets him all emotional. *(Josiah shakes his head sadly. Pause)* Cheer up! ...A bit of palm wine?

Josiah: On empty stomach?

Baba Osa: Try it and see. This is no ordinary palm wine. It is straight from the tree undiluted, a great appetizer. *(He pours into calabash)*

Josiah: Ok.

Baba Osa: Well... *(Very solemnly he lifts his cup)* To the witches and wizards of the market. *(He drops some palm wine)* To mother earth. That swallow up the bones of our colleagues here at home. And to those who joined the whiteman's army, and never came back. Let them rest in peace. Wherever they lay. Be it India, Abysinia, Burma or the high seas. *(He drops palm wine)*

Josiah: Amin, amin.

Baba Osa: Lastly to you and I — our friendship, Josie. *(He drinks a bit and offers the rest to Josiah who drinks it)*

Josiah: Amin, Amin. *(As he takes it and drinks. There is an atmosphere of seriousness during this libation)* (After a short pause) Baba Osa. I am giving up the profession.

32

Baba Osa:	*(Stunned for a moment: then bursts into laughter)* You?...
Josiah:	Me. Fifteen years and I haven't much to show for it. No regrets, of course. But I've made up my mind.
Baba Osa:	*(Seriously)* ...We all give it a thought now and again... Funny, this new girl of mine harps on it all the time. Got any idea what to do at this point?
Josiah:	A lot. I'd tried my hand on a new line — just to raise a capital for other things. In fact that was what landed me in the last trouble.
Baba Osa:	Yes... you said you were in... I swear I never heard about it.
Josiah:	I know... Well, it had nothing to do with the profession... You know when Akin Devil and I broke our partnership, I guess?
Baba Osa:	Over Short Time Mary, wasn't it?
Josiah:	And one or two other things.
Baba Osa:	*(Joking)* Short Time Mary! You boys and women!
Josiah:	Yes. I left the city for Mushin village. There I met one Aliuh "Silver Mother" who invited me to join him in a new venture — pinching army lorries, and equipment. I did so without asking many questions. We had to bribe the sentries, the civilian gatemen, even the European Officer, the mechanics in charge of the depots.
Baba Osa:	That sounds interesting.
Josiah:	Wait! I had invested the little I had, before I heard the horrible facts. The military police were in the habit of knocking an 8-inch nail into the brain of anyone they caught.
Baba Osa:	What? What about the law?

33

Josiah:	The law! Bodies discovered were usually discreetly claimed and buried by relatives of the victims. They sometimes even had to bribe the law not to intervene. How would it sound in society that a kinsman was a lorry thief! He's already dead anyway. It was all a body blow; no cuts, no bruise; only the grunts and the pain as the nail sinks into the brain.
Baba Osa:	That's really terrible. Wicked!
Josiah:	Our first expedition was on a very dark night. It was Easter Monday. The village was merry and we thought we had good cover. As we got close to the army barracks, Aliuh stumbled; he stopped dead. "What's the matter?" I asked. He did not answer me. He just stood there stuck-still, shaking his head. Then he said, "We must go back". Stumbling on the left foot was a bad omen for him!
Baba Osa:	Some people are like that.
Josiah:	We had to cancel the operation for that night. The following day I made up my mind to pull out of the project entirely. So, I went to tell him not to count on me for the next one; and that I wanted my money back. At first he raised no objection. But he went on to say that the money was tied down, and that I had to wait for sometime for my money.
Baba Osa:	Where did this Aliuh come from?
Josiah:	I don't know; he has some funny accent that I couldn't place. Why?
Baba Osa:	O nothing.
Josiah:	Well, I know he was lying about the money being tied down to the project. For, apart from the good luck charm he claimed to have

spent on, bribery was the main part of the budget. And according to him, you had to bribe the personnel where and when you meet them... You just hope you still have enough left when you come across the man with the nails. *(Baba Osa laughs)* So, I took it he was just testing my endurance. He gave me a week.

Baba Osa:	I wonder what is keeping Mugun Yaro?
Josiah:	You're not bored, are you?
Baba Osa:	Not at all.
Josiah:	I went to see Aliuh the following week. He told me I had broken our contract and that I'd lost all my money. As I rushed to handle him, two hefty aides of his pounced on me. Baba Osa! Even Judas Iscariot never suffered compared with me on that morning. The three of them worked on me. They tore everything off me including my trousers and underpants; I had to run into the bush stark naked. Men, women and children were laughing at all sides.
Baba Osa:	Lailah ilailai, Mohamadu Yarsulailai.
Josiah:	But I went back in the evening.
Baba Osa:	I thought you would.
Josiah:	He was having supper with his three wives and children. He rose to meet me. I worked on him with my bejinatu dagger until there was no space left on his face!
Baba Osa:	Josie Atiko, the son of man!
Josiah:	Yes sir! The rest is detail. I got nine months.
Baba Osa:	*(Nods pitifully)* All the money gone!
Josiah:	*(Shrugs affirmatively)* Of course...

35

Baba Osa:	Well, now that I'm really in control here, I plan to set up a whole network throughout the surrounding village markets, with fresh boys. You can come in with me as a supervisor on commission basis. You won't have to lift a finger. That's almost as good as retiring in a way.
Josiah:	*(Thinks)* ...Here?
Baba Osa:	*(Smiling confidently)* Here.
Josiah:	*(Uncertainly)* That's a great thought... But don't you think a clean break is what I need — maybe a breather.
Baba Osa:	Well, in that case you can take a trip to the old village. See your people... give it more thought... Then *(Shrugs)* *(Pause. Then jokingly)* But I bet you won't make a farmer after all these years though!
Josiah:	*(Chuckles)* Not likely! *(We hear bugle, then the sound of a company of soldiers singing and heavy marching is heard approaching. Josiah is startled to alert)*
Josiah:	Soldiers!
Baba Osa:	*(Listens)* Relax. Must be the recruitment campaign again. They haven't been for months. *(Goes towards the window as the sound comes nearer. The singing is in typical lead, chorus and repeat African style)*

Lead: Sah jee – gee – dah
        Sah jee – gee – dah
                    Repeat etc.

Chorus: Hitler matar
         Sah jee gee dah
Odd Voice: *(At intervals)*   'lef righ'
                               'lef righ'

36

	(There is occasional short yodelling by incensed soldiers. Baba Osa nods involuntarily to the marching... Josiah looks troubled)
Baba Osa:	*(Calls him)* ... Only a few of them... Come have a look...
Josiah:	No...
Baba Osa:	Hey! The same officer Mugun Yaro borrowed the looking instrument from... He stands out a whole foot above the rest... Come on... what's the matter with you? *(Josiah rises reluctantly)* You still think they're looking for you, eh? *(Josiah goes nearer the window)* You catch what they're saying? ...They're saying "Hitler's wife should prepare herself ready with sex beads *(laughs)* 'cause they're going to capture both of them... And then..." *(Laughs. Josiah smiles slightly, he is a bit relaxed)*
Josiah:	You speak Hausa?
Baba Osa:	I speak that much...
	(Just then, we hear heavy footsteps approach by the exit followed by three hard aggressive knocks. Josiah freezes; even Baba Osa becomes apprehensive... Baba Osa waves him into the upstage room. He hides the binoculars behind the settee as the knocking is repeated)
Baba Osa:	*(Apprehensively goes to the door)* Who?
Voice:	*(Trying to be friendly)* It's me Baba Osa! *(Baba Osa opens. Enters same police officer we saw earlier in the market scene).*
Baba Osa:	*(Slightly angry and disgusted)* Damn it, it's you Layi ... Knocking like that.
Layi:	*(Forces a nervous smile, ingratiatingly)* I'm sorry, Baba Osa; but it's urgent...

37

Baba Osa:	What is?
Layi:	*(Fumbles)* I mean... well... er... you see... It will be very nice if you give back the loot.
Baba Osa:	What loot?
Layi:	*(Ingratiatingly)*...You know what I'm talking about...
Baba Osa:	I don't.
Layi:	*(Getting more composed)* ...The lavender woman is still at the station crying her eyes out.., her boy's run away with the soldiers on top of it all; she says even her wrapper... *(He stops)* ...Please Baba Osa. I promised to do my best for her.
Baba Osa:	Now assuming I've got some loot, you expect me to hand it over to you just like that? *(Rather impatiently)* Ok... you go. Whatever it is all about, I'll see Bello later.
Layi:	Not possible. Sgt. Bello's gone away; and I'm temporarily in charge while the new sergeant finds his feet... That's the whole point.
Baba Osa:	*(Stunned for a minute, then nods derisively)* And you want to make a quick one in-between... all by yourself eh?
Layi:	Not that. *(Plaintively)* You see, if I recover the loot, it'll go in my service record of Crime Solution. You can always do whatever you like after the new Chief has properly taken charge...
Baba Osa:	What are you people really up to at the station? Not quite two weeks ago, I had to give back a whole box of jewellery for a measly cut of one...
Layi:	That was for Sgt. Bello's client.
Baba Osa:	And this is yours?

Layi:	*(Forgetting himself for a moment. He declares stubbornly)* Record of Crime Solution has to do with promotion papers! *(Baba Osa looked at him with shocked disbelief at his tone and manner. Layi quickly and bashfully makes amend)* I mean I'll arrange for a decent cut for you...
Baba Osa:	*(Smiles and stares at him patronizingly)* ...Grab yourself a drop of palm wine... *(Layi hesitates)* C'mon! *(He is undecided. Baba Osa seizes the initiative and pours him some. He drinks up at a go, evidently against his own will)*
Baba Osa:	*(Taking the calabash from him)* Nice eh? So we have a new sergeant eh? *(Layi nods)* I'm sure you'll get to the bottom of this lavender woman business somehow... In any case, I'll see you later sometimes eh! With your new boss as well... eh! *(Layi is lost for words. He shuffles. He gropes ineffectually. Baba Osa is smiling)* See you later then...
	(Layi backs up uncertainly and exits)
	Greedy fool!
Josiah:	*(Enters cautiously in amazement)* He's gone!
Baba Osa:	He had to.
Josiah:	*(Impressed)* Fantastic. I can't believe it. Now I see what you mean about this place... I never can deal with the police like that... Because I never quite understand them.
Baba Osa:	Who does? You just understand yourself; and take your chances!
Josiah:	Jeri!
Baba Osa:	*(With great confidence)* Jeri Coco!
Josiah:	*(Smiling)* Abumbu Yanya!
Baba Osa:	Water of Alakrity.

39

Josiah:	He go make them sick.
Baba Osa:	*(Triumphantly)* He go make us cure. *(They both laugh and pour more palm wine. Enters Mugun Yaro)* Mugun Yaro, Yaro!
Mugun Yaro:	Yes sir! *(Confidentially to Baba Osa)* I saw him (C/pl Layi) out there; but I ducked.
Baba Osa:	Good lad... *(Examining the dishes. He nibbles)* You must be starving eh?... Sit down and eat. Please carry on, Josiah... I'll examine the barbecue.
Josiah:	I can wait...
Baba Osa:	*(Going)* No, no, carry on... *(Josiah and Mugun eat)*
Josiah:	This is a very delicious sauce. Bush women are famous cooks. *(More chuckles)*
Mugun Yaro:	Sh! sh! *(Confidentially)* She is not a bush woman sir. Master says she was born in the Gold Coast. They sometimes call her Baby Accra.
Josiah:	But she lives here in the bush.
Mugun Yaro:	Yes sir. You said you will take me to the city sir.
Josiah:	Did I? Now why do you want to go to the city?
Mugun Yaro:	To get more civilized and besides I don't like it here. It is only the master that is making me happy. Kids here don't play games with me, and I have to be on my own all the time. But don't tell my master, because he too doesn't like me to mix with other kids in the neighbourhood. He said they will lead me astray.
Josiah:	*(Chuckles)* Tell me, do you want to remain a pickpocket all your life?

Mugun Yaro:	I don't know sir. Perhaps I'll like to become a real robber. But I'm afraid of getting shot like Bramah Daji.
Josiah:	Who is he?
Mugun Yaro:	Bramah Daji was master's friend. He was an Ibariba. He used to talk to me a lot about his night operations. He had plenty of magical power. He could turn to anything; or become invisible in time of danger. But one night he went away, and he never came back *(Confidentially)* They say he was shot with bullets of rice and guinea pepper at Ososun village — in action.
Josiah:	Bullet of rice and guinea pepper? Who told you that?
Mugun Yaro:	Everybody knows it sir. That's the only thing that could get him. He had magic power against all other kinds of bullets.
Josiah:	Un un?
Mugun Yaro:	His people beat their drums and sang sorrowful songs all night. That's what they do whenever anyone of them gets knocked off. They believed he died like a hero and will go on to a higher world of the braves beyond... But don't tell master anything sir.
Josiah:	You really want to go to the city?
Mugun Yaro:	Yes sir.
Josiah:	I can take you to the city, but you won't be allowed to pick pocket.
Mugun Yaro:	What shall I do then?
Josiah:	Well, I can hire you to some big man as a houseboy, and he will send you to school in return for your services. How is that?
Mugun Yaro:	*(Enthusiastically)* School sir?

41

Josiah:	Yes, school.
Mugun Yaro:	That will be very nice. But I can still pick pockets after school hours sir. Can't I?
Josiah:	No, you can't.
Mugun Yaro:	Why not?
Josiah:	Because...er...you see... any kid caught thieving in the city is thrown into the Lagoon with heavy lead round his neck.
Mugun Yaro:	*(Really frightened)* Oh!
Josiah:	Yes, that's the city law.
	(There is a gentle knock. Mugun reacts! Then we hear a feminine voice)
	"It's me..." *(Mugun Yaro opens. Enters Awanatu carrying a huge cloth bag, a huge enamel ware full of odds and ends on her head, and two other small bags. She is gorgeously dressed in African atire: Head-tie, frilled blouse on long skirt of bright imported prints, high-heel shoes, dangling earrings, several bangles, and make up. She is a very young woman of grace and elegance. Somehow, she reminds us of Taiye of Act I. Mugun gives her a hand. She is full of feminine rebellious determination. Josiah is standing in embarrassment. The baggages are discharged)*
Awanatu:	Hello!
Josiah:	Hello! You must be Awanatu.
Awanatu:	*(Trying hard to be polite)* Yes... Where is he?
Mugun Yaro:	In the backyard... *(Shouts upstage to Baba Osa)* She's come, master.
Baba Osa:	...Ok... Coming... *(There follows an awkward silence)*

42

Josiah:	I've heard a lot of good things about you. *(She forces a smile in reply)* ...You do well looking after my friend... I wondered why he's so fit... now I know... Good feeding. *(She smiles genuinely)* Delicious stew is a strong hold on the man *(He laughs a little)* Good cooking captures the heart of a man.
Awanatu:	I do try my best, when I can get hold of him... *(Josiah laughs)* *(Impatiently)* What's he doing out there?
Mugun Yaro:	Barbecue!
Awanatu:	Ruining his appetite again.
Baba Osa:	*(Enters. He evidently had been munching roasted meat. He is in good spirits.)* Eh! Awa my darling queen! *(He notices her mood and the baggages)* What's the matter?
Awanatu:	*(Smiles with feminine recklessness)* I've left him.
Baba Osa:	You what?
Awanatu:	I was here twice to warn you, but you were out...
Baba Osa:	What happened?
Awanatu:	Enough is enough... Anyway he's found out. *(Pause)* We were at it all night long. But he still doesn't know exactly who.
Baba Osa:	*(Thinks, then diverting)* Well... This is Josiah, my friend from the city. *(Josiah smiles formally)*
Awanatu:	He's been very kind... Better have your meal. Mugun said you were very hungry; that's why I rushed things... Your favourites. Asaro with palaver sauce of Kane Fish and shrimps.
Baba Osa:	Very good... Come over here... *(The two get together farthest from the rest. He looks her over)* Did he beat you?

43

Awanatu:	*(Nods)* Only when I refused to name names... I left my own teeth mark on his cheek though.
Baba Osa:	Still... He'll pay for that. You should have mentioned me.
Awanatu:	He said he'll pay soldiers to deal with the person in military fashion. I couldn't bear that...
Baba Osa:	He's only fooling. Soldiers don't play thugs for civilians. ...Did he know you were leaving?
Awanatu:	No. He's still away at work.
Baba Osa:	Good. *(Thinking)* Very good...
Awanatu:	*(Sensing Baba Osa's pre-occupation with questions and answers)* Aren't you glad I came?
Baba Osa:	Of course I am... But we mustn't rush things...
Awanatu:	You said you'll take me away anytime...
Baba Osa:	I know... But we have to play clever... see... buy time, to raise cash *(Kidding)* That's my plan all along. See, now, so you just slip back home before he arrives from work.
Awanatu:	Never!
Baba Osa:	It'll only be for a short time, while I make plans...
Awanatu:	I'm not going back there... I've got to be with you from now on... or...
Baba Osa:	We can't do that right away...
Awanatu:	If you don't want me, then I'll have to find my way to my uncle in Monrovia.
Baba Osa:	Where's that?
Awanatu:	In Liberia... The one free black nation in Africa... That was where I was taking you if you'd pack up your profession.

44

Baba Osa:	*(Vaguely remembering)* O yes! But we can still go there later on. Here, I had a good market. *(Offers her £2 notes)* Go back before he misses you.
Awanatu:	*(Shakes her head)* No, I'd rather end up in some soldiers' barracks until I raise my fare to Monrovia.
Baba Osa:	*(Sternly with forebodden)* Shut up! You must never say that again. Ever!
Awanatu:	*(Recovering from Baba Osa's sharp rebukes, shrugs casually)* What else? *(Pause)* But what ever I do, I'll always want you... I know that for sure.
	(Pause)
Baba Osa:	*(Thinks, and decisively)* Alright. You're not going back to him... I'll set you up in Dende's house round the corner for now .... Until my friend leaves .... How's that?
Awanatu:	That's good .... But what if he comes there?
Baba Osa:	Then I'll show him that I control this town .... You know that, don't you?
Awanatu:	Yes I do. *(She sobs and buries her face in Baba Osa's chest. He embraces, and caresses her gently smiling at his own self-importance. He breaks from her and lifts her chin up gently. Their eyes meet engagingly).*
Baba Osa:	*(Amorously)* My Baby Accra!
Awanatu:	*(Smiling seductively)* Hum!
Baba Osa:	Come on, lets go in for a chat ....
Awanatu:	*(Gently)* No. Go eat your meal first.
Baba Osa:	That can wait ....
	(Very gentle romantic struggle between the two)

Awanatu:	No .... Your friend is here .... Not now.
	(We hear three loud aggressive knocks. They are shocked to alertness. He ushers Awanatu into the room; giving her the unceremoniously as she goes).
Baba Osa:	*(Angry)* Is that you, Layi?
Voice:	*(Knocks)* Open up in the name of the Government! Open up!
Baba Osa:	Alright! Alright! What's all the banging about?
Layi:	*(Ignoring Baba Osa, he rushes in to take a prominent position like a kid playing games. He is laden with baton and two handcuffs. He had worked himself up to this pitch)* Stay still, everybody! This is a raid!
Baba Osa:	*(Bursts into loud laughter)* What raid? What's the matter with you?
Layi:	You know what is the matter. You are coming to the station with me, now.
Baba Osa:	Me? Come on, calm down; and show me a bit of respect eh!
Layi:	*(Declamatorily)* The law is no respector of persons!
Baba Osa:	*(Smiles)* Oh yeah?
Layi:	*(Still breathing heavily)* Where were you this morning?
Baba Osa:	*(Incredulous)* Where was I this morning?
Layi:	*(Picks more courage)* You are repeating my question. *(Pause)* I'm taking you in for stealing in the market this morning. I don't want to use these handcuffs. You see I have got them, in case. *(He rattles the handcuffs)*
Baba Osa:	*(Sternly)* Now don't over-do things. Go back to the station. Tell the Sergeant I'll see him later.

46

Layi:	You are not seeing anyone later.... I am in charge of this case.
Baba Osa:	*(Really angry)* Quit being childish, I'm being civil with you and you are still carrying on; what have you got on me? I can see my familiarity with you is breeding contempt.
Layi:	This time I have plenty on you. There is a reliable eye-witness waiting to testify against you and your little rat, who is struggling with fish bones over there. *(Reference to Mugun, who is eating, unconcerned)*
Mugun Yaro:	*(Startled)* Who? Me sir?
Layi:	Yes, you little rat of the market.
Mugun Yaro:	I have never left this house today, sir.
Baba Osa:	Leave the kid out of it and get out of here before I throw you out!
Layi:	You dare touch the Government's uniform... and you'll be away for fifteen years .... *(Baba Osa laughs uneasily)*.
Josiah:	I just can't sit here watching you two. You sound like two old pals to me .... Why don't you cool temper and talk talkie eh.
Baba Osa:	*(To Josiah)* I take that point .... Now Layi ....
Layi:	*(Interrupts vehemently)* Corporal Layi!
Baba Osa:	*(Smiles condescendingly)* Ok the Corporal Layi. *(Moving away from the rest, he beckons to Layi for a tete-a-tete)* Over here!
Layi:	What's the secrecy? Speak to me here in the open.
Baba Osa:	*(Angry and shouting indignantly)* Alright. I'm telling you I've done no operation today. But if you're so broke you lose your self respect ... your composure as a constable in my house, I'll fix you up for now!

47

Layi:	*(Stubbornly)* The Lavender woman is still at the station!
Baba Osa:	*(Smiles, shaking his head)* O' God .... What exactly is your need?
Layi:	*(Thinks as he shuffles nervously)* You are making the offer.
Baba Osa:	You know, I'm still to meet your new boss.
Layi:	That's no concern of mine.
Baba Osa:	*(Laughs heartily)* Showing off in front of my friend eh! *(Layi keeps up his tension without a word)*
Baba Osa:	*(Forced smile)* Ok. You wait here a minute. *(On his way to the room, he stops to take an amused look at Layi)* Relax! Sit down and wet your throat!
Layi:	*(Swallows hard)* I am on duty! *(Baba Osa laughs and exits to the room)*
	(Striding around pompously, clicking heels and jingling the handcuffs) God knows what goes on in this den ... with barbecue roasting in the backyard and all .... *(Muttering)* We'll see about that one later ... *(Curiously to Josiah)* I see you're new to this part, mister? *(Josiah smiles disarmingly)* ... What's going on there, Baba Osa? I haven't got all day.
Baba Osa:	*(Off stage)* Shut up, will you! *(Enters)* This is your big *pay day* Corporal Layi. Here. For you alone. *(He offers two pound notes. Policeman takes pound notes and simultaneously blows his whistle with vigour. The Sergeant Momo bursts in, pushing the door with violence, blowing his own whistle)*
Sgt. Momo:	Stay still, everybody. (Layi wrestles with Baba Osa).

Layi:	(Out of breath, as he struggles with Baba Osa) He tries to bribe me Serge! (He crashes to the floor and groans under Baba Osa). He grabs my member Sergeant. He grabs me! hm ...uh .... (Baba Osa is squeezing life out of Layi)
Sgt. Momo:	He'll get an extra charge for that. (Joins in the struggle to overpower Baba Osa).
Mugun Yaro:	(Starts crying) They want to kill my master! Oh God they want to kill him. (The struggle continues on the floor).
Josiah:	(Restraining himself from joining in) You know, you have no right to do this to him in his own house. You know you have no right, Sergeant!
Sgt. Momo:	You wait for your turn lawyer (Amidst the struggle comes the clicking of the handcuffs).
Baba Osa:	(Breathing heavily) You two are crazy ... attacking me in my own house!
Sgt. Momo:	You are under arrest! (Seizes the money) Now where is the rest?
Baba Osa:	The rest of what?
Layi:	Must be in that room somewhere, Serg.
Sgt. Momo:	Get it!
	(Layi goes into Baba Osa's room)
Baba Osa:	Don't enter my room. You have no warrant, you hear that?
	(Noise of ransacking emanates from the room)
Sgt. Momo:	I need no warrant for the like of you. I'm here to put an end to all the nonsense that goes on in this town. And by God, I'll do it as my name is Momo.
Josiah:	(Impulsively) Momo!

49

Sgt. Momo:	*(Pompously)* Yes, Senior Sgt. R.R.W. Momo, late of the Criminal Investigation Department in the city. *(Stares at Josiah)* ... Don't I know you somewhere.
Josiah:	No ... not me.
Baba Osa:	You can't bluff me. You have no warrant ....
Layi:	*(Enters with a bag)* I've got it .... Serg. It is just as the woman said....
Baba Osa:	Don't tamper with my personal savings!
Sgt. Momo:	*(Takes the bag)* Anything else Corporal?
Layi:	*(Hesitates, then rushes into room and brings back the army sweater)* Government property!
Sgt. Momo:	Good .... You love the army uniform eh ... very good!
Baba Osa:	I don't know what you're talking about.
Layi:	*(Triumphantly)* We've got the Big fish hooked, Serg....
Sgt. Momo:	All credits to you, Corporal. *(Layi salutes smartly)* Lets go!
Baba Osa:	Eh ...Sergeant! *(Pleading)* Please, can I have a word with my friend about my belongings and other little matters?
Sgt. Momo:	*(Hesitates)* Alright, make it snappy; and stay in view.
	(Baba Osa and Josiah confer aside). The others watch them as Baba Osa whispers and Josiah nods in agreement.)
Layi:	They are saying something funny, Serg.
Sgt. Momo:	Ok. That's enough chattering there, you two.
Layi:	*(Moves in on the two)* You heard the Sergeant!
Baba Osa:	*(Cool and deliberately)* Corporal Layi.

50

Layi:	Yes.
Baba Osa:	*(Licks little finger)* You'll never be a sergeant!
Layi:	*(Alarmed)* O' God! You hear that Serg! He put his little finger in his mouth before he said it, Serg. Curse, magic.
Sgt. Momo:	Don't worry about it: he is not on Police Promotion Board, is he?
Layi:	No Serg. But he'll pay for that *(Tears a button from his shirt and holds it aloft)* Now you are also in for malicious damage to government property on the person of a law-enforcing officer! *(Looks eagerly at Sgt. for approval)*
Sgt. Momo:	*(Irritated)* Keep your button, Corporal!
Layi:	Yes Serg. *(Humbly pockets his button)*.
Sgt. Momo:	Off we go. *(They are at the door when Baba Osa casually turns around to face his assistants. The officers are curious)*.
Baba Osa:	*(With usual authority)* Mugun Yaro!
Mugun Yaro:	Sir!
Baba Osa:	Be a man, Mugun; always be a man.
Mugun Yaro:	*(Obediently, with emotion)* Yes sir!
Josiah:	Sea never dry!
Baba Osa:	*(With slight smile)* Butterfly shall never fall over! *(The two officers had been caught unaware. They seem carried away by a curious interest in the cross-talk, until Baba Osa addresses them with calm authority)* Let's go gentlemen.
	(They are all gone, leaving Josiah and Mugun Yaro with Awanatu still in the room)
Mugun Yaro:	*(In tears)* They are going to lock up my master.
Josiah:	You keep quiet and start packing your things.
Mugun Yaro:	Yes sir ... nothing to pack anyway ....

51

Awanatu:	*(Approaching from room in very agitated state)* They have taken him away. I heard everything. What are we going to do?
Josiah:	You just do as I say. Clear your things away and come back immediately to lock up the place. Baba Osa will be in touch with you later.
Awanatu:	*(Suspicious)* When is later?
Josiah:	Never mind ....
Awanatu:	*(Infuriated)* Never mind! .... Never mind. Your friend got arrested right in front of you and all you can think of is run away—taking his assistant with you.
Josiah:	Baba Osa will explain everything to you later.
Awanatu:	Yes indeed, when he rots in prison. Mugun Yaro; will you desert your master or will you stay here and let me look after you? Answer me.
Mugun Yaro:	*(Confused)* I .... I ....
Josiah:	Oh women! We have no time for all this; but listen.
Awanatu:	Listen to what?
Josiah:	You must have heard the police saying there is some eye-witness waiting at the station, besides the lavender woman herself. But the thing is, Baba Osa did not take part in person: Mugun and I pulled the job. That's why he asks both of us to disappear for now; because they'll be back here the minute they realize their mistake ... It's the only chance all round .... Satisfied?
Awanatu:	*(Trying to understand)* Why didn't you say that at first?

Josiah:	Better you lock up right now.
Awanatu:	*(Starts to pack her utensils, and then stops to think)* Suppose they still lock him up after all.
Josiah:	One doesn't think on those lines in the profession, little sister: otherwise *we don't ever lift* a finger .... *(Noticing she is a bit alarmed, he puts a hand on her shoulder tenderly)* In the style of a top professional, he's done his best. It is for you and I to hope for the best.
	(Pause, as the reality sinks in)
Awanatu:	*(Nods gently)* Alright.
Josiah:	Ready, Mugun?
Mugun Yaro:	Ready sir. O! the barbecue!
Josiah:	Never mind that, greedy. Let's get out of here. *(Distant train blows a long one in full motion).*
Awanatu:	You'll keep in touch Mugun, won't you?
Mugun Yaro:	I will... My money box! *(He grabs it from under the settee and shakes it instinctively)*
Josiah:	Remember, Awanatu, you have seen nothing, you have heard nothing. Goodbye for now.
Awanatu:	*(Almost in tears. She nods in response)* Goodbye Mugun!
Mugun Yaro:	Goodbye.
Josiah:	If we catch that train, you'll have supper in the city tonight.
Mugun Yaro:	The city?
Josiah:	Yes, the city. C'mon.
	(The two are about to exit when we hear the marching of soldiers singing a different song this time. Josiah and Awanatu listen with

53

	diverse interests, Mugun looks from one to another)
Mugun Yaro:	Soldiers!
Lead:	Laih lah Lahih lah — nlah!
Chorus:	*(Repeat as above)*
Lead:	Laih Leh Halih — lah — nlah!
Chorus:	*(Repeat as above)*
Lead:	Laih — Lah Hahih — lan - lah! Mohamadoo — Yarah Suh - lih - lah!
Chorus:	*(Repeat as above)*
Lead:	Lalh — lah Haluh — lah
Chorus:	*(Repeat as above and so on)*

(Josiah thinks first of his escape: then of actually joining up... Awanatu momentarily snaps out of her sadness over Baba Osa, to think of her possibilities with the soldiers. Mugun feels the two are thinking about what he does not quite understand. Josiah makes the decision)

Josiah:	Let's go, kid.

(He grabs Mugun, who waves to Awanatu as the two exit. The soldiers song continues. Awanatu is packing her things as ...)

CURTAIN

54

A Man named Mokai

Characters

Towncrier
Man
Mokai
General
The Flock: Emily
                        Iya'jo
                        Pastor
                        Derin
                        Titi
                        Uzo
1st Cult Leader
2nd Cult Leader
Young Cultman
Cultmen *(4 upward)*
Lieutenant
Soldiers *(4 upward)*
Revolutionary Association
of Tough Soldiers (RATS)
RATS (4 upward)
Major Ndem
Professor Tomwuruwuru
Assistant

Scene I

House lights still on.

Lead Chanter: Riwo, riwo yah!
Riwo yah! Riwo yeá! yeá!!

Chorus: *(Repeat above, all vigorously. They continue —
lead and chorus until fade out)*
*Actors enters from the aisles dancing, jumping,
chanting, cheering, greetings to audience on to
the stage and troop off.*
Black out
*Lights go up on a bare stage suggesting an
opening in one part of the village. We hear
towncrier's voice.*

Towncrier : Our story starts here, in the village of Akilagun,
about a man named MOKAI. *(He calls "lights!"
Lights change to night on bare stage, suggesting
open space in the village. Towncrier in character,
hits gong)*

Come ye all *(Gong)*
Come listen *(Gong)*
Come ye all
Come listen
The Chief greets you all
The elders greet you all
Some kind of breeze is blowing
Over us in Akilagun; it's blowing
it's blowing
It doesn't stop
It must stop.
Now the High Priest has made the decision
So, if you lose a goat: search;
a sheep: search;
a chicken... search.

57

But a human being: don't.

(He is interrupted by the appearance of Man)

Man:	Hey Towncrier. What's up?
Towncrier:	If you don't interrupt me, you will **hear it**.
Man:	Tell us then.
Towncrier:	You've made me lose my rhythm. I must **start all** over again. *(He starts with gong)* Come ye all... *(Gong)*... Come listen.
Man:	Just tell us...
Towncrier:	There you go again. Think towncrying is a private conversation, eh?
Man:	Alright, never mind the message. We'll all get to know it anyway... *(Indicating his mate)* This man here is looking for his mother's people.
Towncrier:	What?
Man:	His mother's people!... He thinks somebody might know them around here. So, naturally...
Towncrier:	*(Eyes the other suspiciously)* His mother's people! Why doesn't he ask his father's people about his mother's people?
Man:	Serious!
Towncrier:	*(Peers through Mokai)* You two having me on? A big man like this. *(Realising)* Eh! I haven't seen you here before, have I?
Mokai:	Not likely, I'm a stranger here...
Towncrier:	*(Getting sinisterly interested)* Stranger, are you?
Man:	He's told you. Can you help him or not?
Towncrier:	*(Scheming)* Maybe I can... Yes, I think I can. *(To Man)* You may go, I'll do my best for him...
Man:	That's better... *(To Mokai)* He knows everything around here... Bye, stranger. *(He exits)*
Towncrier:	He's right... Now... who may your mother's people be?

Mokai:	*(Puzzled by the Towncrier's sudden interest)* Well... it all started from the little cottage at the edge of the Savannah...
Towncrier:	What cottage?
Mokai:	Some place far, far away...
	(Noise of multitude offstage. Towncrier's interest switches to the noise)
Towncrier:	Wait... You're looking for your mother's people, are you?... You'll find them here alright. *(He starts beating his gong vigorously and bellows)* 'Ye eh 'Eran a ke e!' *(Sacrificial meat is here).*
	(Mokai is momentarily confused. The noise offstage sounds nearer aggressively)
Mokai:	*(Alarmed)* What's that?
Towncrier:	*(Sarcastically)* Your mother's people... coming. *(Mokai makes a start)* Don't move!
	(Mokai starts. Towncrier drops his gong and makes for Mokai, who knocks him off, in time to run for it. The crowd enter and chase after him. The crowd all wear loin-clothes and white paint on their faces. Drum and chant. They chase him round the stage until Mokai escapes. They continue. We hear Mokai's moaning protest).
	(Jubilating) Fancy that!... Eh! From Crier to a catcher. *(He goes in the opposite direction of the crowd).*

FADE OUT WITH DRUMMING AND CHANTING

Two Guards at Altar.

Slow fade-in as music subsides. Only incessant drum-beats continue. Two men stand watching over an altar that looks like an anthill. In front of the altar sits a man **(Mokai)** *in a coiled position with his head between his thighs. He is dead still. One of the Guards appears restless. He looks to and fro. He peers at the man by the altar.*

2nd Guard:	Rather cheap the way they got him, wasn't it?
1st Guard:	The Towncrier did it.
2nd Guard:	**Caught by a mere Towncrier!** *(He looks expectantly in the direction of the man)* This place is doleful. *(Pause)* I wonder how long we have to wait, for the High Priest.
1st Guard:	You know he won't come until the moon is up here.
2nd Guard:	*(Sarcastic)* Shout to the moon to come up. *(Indicating the victim)* Poor thing!
1st Guard:	Will you stop that? *(Silence. Peers at Mokai who is crouching with his head tucked in still)* Odd isn't it? A man with such strength getting trapped by the Towncrier!
2nd Guard:	But the trouble he gave the Elders later!
1st Guard:	I hear they had to hit him on the neck with Aluwo club before they could take his mind away.
2nd Guard:	He was still jabbering on after that.
1st Guard:	Where did he come from?
2nd Guard:	Nobody knows, not a single mark on him to tell a tale.
1st Guard:	Could be some stray robber... or a hack mystic.
2nd Guard:	Weird. *(Remembering)* Funny thing though! He bears some strange resemblance to the High Priest himself... I mean his eyes. They twinkle, and then winkle at times.

1st Guard:	I saw him when he was trapped. But I didn't notice a thing like that.
2nd Guard:	Everybody saw it.
1st Guard:	Who's everybody?
2nd Guard:	Everybody. Even High Priest himself kept avoiding the man's gaze. Everybody saw that too.
1st Guard:	*(Mimics)* Everybody, everybody! Better stop it!
2nd Guard:	Don't shout at me.
1st Guard:	You are frightened.
2nd Guard:	Yes, I am frightened.
1st Guard:	You volunteered.
2nd Guard:	Yes... it was supposed to be a goat at first. Now *(indicating man)*... him!
1st Guard:	What's the difference. It's for the High Priest to decide what he wants for the gods, isn't it?
2nd Guard:	I just hope the government in the city doesn't get to know about it.
1st Guard:	*(Contemptuous)* Government! The Cult is becoming something else with people like you in it. Better go home to mother for your milk.
2nd Guard:	Don't insult me.
1st Guard:	Then keep quiet.
	(Brief silence)
	I wonder who will succeed the High Priest when the time comes...
2nd Guard:	They'll have to look among his cousins.
1st Guard:	The end of a line. Pity that.
2nd Guard:	Pity nothing. Good riddance.
1st Guard:	Watch your mouth.
2nd Guard:	All this misfortune in his time, eh?
1st Guard:	What could he do about it?

61

2nd Guard:	All these many autumns; and not a single season you could really call harvest!
1st Guard:	The will of the gods.
2nd Guard:	People say it has got to do with the High Priest. The pranks and the awful things he'd done in his time.
1st Guard:	*(Admonishing)* Gossip of malice.
2nd Guard:	*(Shrugs)* Alright, it's gossip then.
1st Guard:	C'mon, what do you know?
2nd Guard:	You said it's gossip...
1st Guard:	C'mon. Tell me.
2nd Guard:	You are trying to trap me.
1st Guard:	No. Cult to Cult. Your word is my death. *(Makes sign: clenched fist on his chest)*
2nd Guard:	*(Confidentially)* A sacrilege: real abomination. It was hushed up, but the story went around none-the-less. A man putting his foot in his mouth.
1st Guard:	How?
2nd Guard:	*(Looks left and right for security)* They say he broke into the grove, removed the ceremonial masks of the ancestors and distributed them among his mates. Then he led them into the bush to attack some innocent maiden of the village...
1st Guard:	No!
2nd Guard:	Yes. And that on the eve of the arrival of the ancestors!
1st Guard:	Who told you all these?
2nd Guard:	You ask me that!
1st Guard:	Who was this maiden?
2nd Guard:	How would I know? I mean the whole thing happened such a long time ago.

1st Guard:	Such story!
2nd Guard:	There are more, but that was the worst.
1st Guard:	And he was allowed to become the High Priest!
2nd Guard:	Cult was backing-up the Cult at all events.
1st Guard:	And that's why we have no harvest!
2nd Guard:	Not since he took over. At least you know that.
1st Guard:	I hope he *(indicating victim)* can change all that...
2nd Guard:	I hope he does too. But I wish the High Priest would come and get it over with.
1st Guard:	How can he come without the supreme witness?
2nd Guard:	The moon! I wish the moon will go up.
1st Guard:	*(Comforting)* Relax.
2nd Guard:	I can't.
1st Guard:	*(Poking fun)* This must be your first of this kind.
2nd Guard:	Yes, and I hope it is my last.
1st Guard:	Sh!! Sh!!

We hear slow beats of the drum off-stage. Simultaneously the moon effect appears gradually to illuminate the stage.

63

Scene II

High Priest enters with staff of office doing slow, quick slow, quick slow... dance movement. Two steps forward, one backward.
He is supported by two henchmen. The High Priest wears a grotesque mask and elaborate headgear. High Priest stops music with arm raised.

High Priest: *(Saluting the victim thus)* Oto! Tonight is the night of the gods.

Guards repeat each line after High Priest in unison.

The moon has come to be our witness.

Guards: The moon has come to be our witness.

High Priest: We have brought you the chosen one to carry away the autumn.

Guards: We have brought you the chosen one to carry back the harvest.

High Priest: *(To victim)*

You are the chosen one.
Tonight is your night.
The moon shall not compete with you tonight.
The fairies of the forest
Shall not compete with you tonight.
The mothers of the earth
Shall not share with you tonight.
You are the chosen one;
Tonight is your night.
I command you to rise.
High to your Grandnight.

Crescendo of drumming.

High Priest:	(Chanting)	
	B'ewure ba bimo loojo	New born goat
	Omo rè a dide e e!	Never fails to rise.
		On the day of birth.
	Kó didee, Ko dide o	Rise! rise!! rise!!!
		You must rise.
	B'agutan ba bimo loojo	New born sheep
	Omo re a si dagbà à à!	Never fails to rise
		On the day of birth.
	Ko didee, Ko dide o	You must rise.

Others: *(Swaying and stepping side to side to drumming and chanting in unison to slow beat)*

Eru gale k'o dide o.

High Priest: Kodide é é. Ko dide o.

Others: Eru gale k'o dide o.

The victim stirs noticeably. The High Priest appears triumphant, shouting:

Dide! Dide! 'o.	Rise! Rise! Rise!
	The word is rise!
	Never fail to rise!
	Rise! Rise!! Rise!!!

Chorus: Eru gale k'o dide o.

Drum-beat from off-stage becomes vigorous. The High Priest seems possessed as he shouts to Guards, "Now". They ceremonially give him a large cutlass. They all exit. He prances round the victim; dances ceremonially, brandishing the cutlass. The victim is stirring like a rose petal. High Priest directs him to lay on the altar, but the victim moves towards him menacingly like a robot.

High Priest is backing round the altar saying incantations to control the victim; but without effect. High Priest yells and the drumbeats stop. Victim engages him in combat. Others chant from off-stage without drumming.

Se're, se re,	Perform the ritual right;
Ajiborisa, se re,	High Priest
Se re, se re	Perform the ritual right.
Ajiborisa, se re.	

Victim overpowers High Priest and escapes. High Priest is dazed and feels disgraced. Substituting himself for the victim he puts the dagger through himself and dies on the altar.

An assistant enters with bowl. He sees the High Priest lying still; dead. He drops his calabash, backs up shouting "Oo roo", and runs off.

There is commotion off-stage. Crowd enter, some carrying off the dead High Priest while others pursue Mokai. Angry ominous drumbeats take over.
Mokai re-enters from another direction and runs off as lights fade out. Drum continues.

Scene changes.

Olifie

Lights come up slowly with very distant reports of gunfire. This is the cemetery end of Mount Olifie Village Church. It is dawn. Mokai lies asleep. He is disturbed by the noise. He stirs and rolls, but sleeps on. Emily, a young woman carrying a water pot, enters. She peers at Mokai and hurries off in fright. After a while, a man enters stealthily. He is dishevelled and rather bewildered. He wears an Army General's uniform but with canvass shoes. His trousers are rolled up, obviously to facilitate fast movement in the woods. He tiptoes towards Mokai, pauses a while, and begins to seize Mokai's bundle of clothes. Mokai wakes and a tussle begins. The man doesn't say a word, but struggles on. Mokai wrenches the clothes back from the man. A brief struggle leaves the man sprawling. The man gives up, rises. The

66

	two men back away from each other speechless: *the man's gesture is apologetic.)*
Gen / Man:	*(Pleads)*I need that, man... I need it badly.
	(No answer.)
	You're not dumb... *(Desperate)* Trouble. Real trouble, Mister... (Voices come from offstage) I'll pay you for it.
Lead:	Holy!
Rest:	Holy! Holy!! Holy!!!
Gen / Man:	*(Starts)* Give it me... I'll repay you, please. *(He fumbles in his pocket)*This is the place of the dead... I'll be dead if... *More voices. Gen / Man is pulling away. He runs off.*
	Enter a group of women led by Emily. They are dressed in white cotton gowns and caps. They all stop. Mokai senses them.
Iya'jo:	Eh you there?
	Mokai shakes his head desperately, but he is unable to find his voice. He points in some direction vigorously and gasps in an attempt to speak. He finally gives up.at the edge of tears,
Emily:	He's a mute.
Iya'jo:	*(to others)* Quick, tell the pastor... of the evil spirit... Quick!
	(One of the girls goes)
	This one spoke once.
	(Mokai nods affirmatively and tries in vain to speak)
Ija'jo:	Speak!
Emily:	He can't.

Iya'jo:	He will. *(Notices the garment Mokai is clutching)* Is that yours? Where did you get it from?
	(Mokai feels the cloth. He seems emotionally charged but unable to say a word)
	Alright, alright, forget. *(To others)* Better let him forget.
	(Enter Pastor and the errand-girl. He carries a big cross while the errand-girl carries candles, incense and burner. Iya'jo hurries to meet him)
	(Reverently) Master, your vision has come true on the eve of Pentecost!
	(She whispers to Pastor about her opinion and suspicion of Mokai's condition. The two are in accord. During this, Emily rather impulsively goes close to Mokai for a look and touch)
	(Shouts) Keep off! *(Remonstrating)* Discipline, child!
	(Emily bows regretfully and backs away)
Pastor:	*(With arms raised towards Mokai)*
	Peace!
	Peace be unto you, stranger.
	It has been revealed to us
	from high and above
	that you shall arrive
	to seek sanctuary on Olifie!
Rest:	*(Together)* Holy! Holy!! Holy!!!
Pastor:	We sensed you
	As you roll towards
	This holy portion of earth
	In search of Peace.
All:	Holy! Holy!! Holy!!!
Pastor:	Thou hast reached the Sanctuary
	Of the Flock of Jehova
	On the Hill of Olifie!

All:	Holy! Holy!! Holy!!!
Pastor:	*(To flock)*
	Lambs of Olifie
	Welcome the wandering lamb into the fold.
All:	*(Arms outstretched)*
	Welcome, welcome
	Lamb of the Lord
	Welcome into the fold.
Pastor:	The Lord calleth thee... today, on the eve of the Feast of Pentecost.
All:	And thou cometh,
	In His name
	Most high, most venerable
	Today on the eve of Pentecost.
Pastor:	*(Points staff to Mokai who kneels instinctively)*
	Here shalt thou stay
	To fulfil thy destiny
	On earth and the world beyond.
	Welcome, welcome
	Lamb of the Lord
	Welcome into this
	Holy portion of earth!
	You shall S-P-E-A-K!
	In the name of the Lord, you shall S-P-E-A-K.
All:	Holy! Holy!! Holy!!!
	(Mokai is making gasping effort to speak. He is moving towards Pastor on his knees with outstretched arms. He is swaying in rhythm with the rest)
Mokai:	*(Mouthing)* Holy! Holy!! Holy!!!
Pastor:	*(Putting staff on Mokai)*
	Speak, speak, speak
	In the name of
	Jah Jah Jah

69

Seth Seth Senseth
Sham Sham Rago
Eti o feeti
Ludo Ludo Ludo
Ludo Ludo Ludo
Ajagun mo – la-ta a-a-bi!!!

The Rest: Holy!!!

*(The rest now repeat after Pastor. Mokai
has begun to form words albeit involuntarily. He
offers his bundle to Pastor who picks it with his
staff and stamps his foot on it)*

HQ Horta   Venock

Pastor: Vegadoro   Temetia   *(Pandemonium)*
Agola   Rabur
Goth   Emmanuel   *(Individuals say*
Othie   Sabaoth   *various words in*
Adoney   *trance mostly* '**Holy**')

Tetragramaton
Amacor
Amacor
Amides *(Mokai repeats aloud words in trance)*
Alpha et om-e-ga.

All: Halleluia! Halleluia!! Halleluia!!!

*(Mokai is possessed. He continues to say words
accompanying Pastor. He is on his feet. Pastor is
triumphant)*

Pastor: Halleluia! *(Repeat)*

All: Halleluia!

*(Mokai raises his hands up saying all sorts of
words similar, but not the same, as Pastor. Pastor
and the rest now wait for Mokai to stop, but he
gets stonger. Emily suddenly rushes to grab
Mokai petting him and shouting)*

Emily: Holy, Holy, Holy... (etc)

Mokai rants on. Pastor looks helpless.

Pastor:	*(Decisively)* Stop! Stop! I say stop in the name of the Almighty. Stop!
	(Mokai continues)
Emily:	*(Drops to her knees clutching at Mokai's thigh rolling, fully possessed and shouting)* Holy, Holy, Holy (etc)
All (Except Pastor):	Halleluia!
Pastor:	Enough! Stranger, I say enough!
	(The act continues)
	Emily, get back into line.
	(No effect)
	Emily! Emily! *(Turns to Mokai)* Stranger, I say stop!
All:	Halleluia!... Holy...
	(Pastor struggles to control the situation. One by one the rest join in holy words)
Pastor:	*(Desperately pleads to flock)* Wait for Pentecost! Tomorrow is Pentecost... wait till tomorrow... Iya'jo Pentecost! *(He grabs Iya'jo, shouts)* Pentecost!
	(Iya'jo comes gradually out of possession but very bewildered while the others continue. Pastor encouraged by his success with Iya'jo, appeals to the rest)
	Stop, O lambs of Olifie. Tomorrow is Pentecost Tomorrow is Pentecost Omega, Omega, Omega.
	(The flock stop severally and Mokai last. They are all completely bewildered, still in trance)
Iya'jo:	*(To Pastor)* Master, your vision, your *prophecy* has come to pass.
	(Black out)

Days Later
Mokai/Emily
Lights up.

(Enter Emily. She looks round, sees someone off-stage and calls)

Emily: *(Secretively)* Mokai... Mokai! Glory be.

Mokai: *(Entering)* Glory be, Emily... *(Sulking)* What do you want?

Emily: Sisi Lagos was looking for you.

Mokai: She can wait.

Emily: She is on her way back to the city. Pastor doesn't want her around. I'd say good riddance.

Mokai: *(Still sulking)* She's gone then.

Emily: Banished. I have been looking for you all over the place. You are so cold. What's the matter?

Mokai: Nothing.

Emily: C'mon. The Meek One of the Lord.

Mokai: Go back to the flock to finish the Lord's Supper.

Emily: It's over.

Mokai: Go lick the pulpit; and pyx; and the transept, the ambry; the glebe and the baldachin, and the transforium and...

Emily: *(Puts hand gently over his mouth)* Alright, alright. I'm sorry you were locked out of the Lord's Supper. It's because you are not confirmed as yet.

Mokai: I'm not good enough. I cut the grass, I clean the church, bathe the candles, prepare the Lord's Supper, but when it's time to eat it... I get locked out...

Emily: It's just a simple ceremony.

Mokai: When you all gather round and eat up the Lord's Supper, we shall see what the Lord himself will bite before going to bed.

72

Emily:	(Laughs) Such joke: such sense of humour! You have' more in you than ten confirmations put together.
Mokai:	What is that?
Emily:	Your gift... Like the performance you gave on the eve of the Feast of Pentecost... and again at the funeral of Papa Abel.
Mokai:	(Frowns) Me?
Emily:	When the coffin was being laid to rest and you suddenly burst into all those holy words which no-one, not even the Pastor, could make out...
Mokai:	O' that!
Emily:	And the vision... (Admiring) Oh... the whole of Olifie is still talking about it: even at the Lord's Supper. (Pause) Please Mokai, could you tell me the meaning of those words?
Mokai:	I don't know.
Emily:	You don't know? You said an event of great magnitude will occur in Olifie. You kept repeating it in between the holy words...
Mokai:	I don't remember, Emily.
Emily:	(Concerned) You must... try...
Mokai:	I can't.
Emily:	(Puzzled) Could it be the Pastor was right?
Mokai:	He's never wrong.
Emily:	(Gossiping) Ugh! You don't know him. He'd started on you right on the eve of Pentecost. He thought you were making things up. Then at the funeral of Papa Abel, after all the holy words had come out of you, he said you had Belzeebub!
Mokai:	(Scandalised) Me? Belzeebub?
Emily:	Keep calm. I don't believe him. Iya'jo doesn't either. See, you have your own followers.

73

Mokai:	*(Thinks)* Now, now, I don't want to divide Olifie. I met it intact.
Emily:	Save yourself. Nothing was intact here at Olifie. *(Confidentially)* Of late, Pastor tried to marry Iya'jo off with Papa Abel, it didn't work out. Then he himself went after Sisi Lagos right from the moment she arrived from the city with her husband. She came asking the Lord for a child. But when Pastor stepped in... The poor man went back swearing he'll get Pastor any day of the Lord... Now Pastor's banished Sisi Lagos... for your sake! *(Lovingly)* It's good you came, Mokai; life was empty before you came. It's always been sing, dance and worship and... *(She stops herself)* ... perhaps wait for death and heaven! Look around. *(Pointing to graves)* You see it happened to Papa Abel; right before your own eyes. He was the Sexton, true to God and man on Olifie... cleaned the church... rang the bell... cut the lawn and tilled the Lord's piece of land for Pastor to plant and grow tomatoes and vegetables. In fact he did all the jobs you now inherit. *(With a touch of irony)* And like you, he never got to eat the Lord's Supper. He just fell off and died... *(Smiling)* as if he was waiting for you to arrive.
Mokai:	*(Alarmed)* What are you getting at? *(Getting excited)* I see. That's it, he? That's what he's planning... He made me Sexton... calling me the Meek One of the Lord...
Emily:	He's got us all. Before you came along *(She moves tenderly close to Mokai)* ... before you came along... O' Mokai... *(She moves close to him)* Loneliness before you came along... O'.
Mokai:	*(Exasperated)* He said I have Belzeebub! He taught me your ways... At midnight of the Feast of Pentecost, he took me

74

round the cemetery. We counted the graves. He
said the dead are in majority without voice in
Olifie. And if I'd like to be their spokesman. I
said, yes.

Emily: A medium!

Mokai: He said I was the Chosen One. I slept in the
church. I fasted. I have been sleeping on Papa
Abel's grave since the night of Pentecost. And
now, he turned round to say I have Belzeebub.

Emily: He made you sleep on Papa Abel's grave?

Mokai: *(Justifying)* I agreed to it. The only way to get the
voice of the majority... *(Sulking)* He said I have
Belzeebub.

Emily: Forget Belzeebub! You got any message from the
dead?

Mokai: No message... apart from the great event that
will occur in Olifie...

Emily: *(Glowing)* The great event! Ah! You said that
before. I will be here to see it... With you! O' come
(She pulls him) ... let's get away... C'mon.

Mokai: Where to?

Emily: To the river... *(Offers her hand)* Take me to the
river.

Mokai: To help you out.

Emily: No, just to talk. Talk by the riverside. You and I
are one now.

Mokai: How's that?

Emily: Holy union. The shell and the snail... Until
death do us...

Mokai: *(Interrupts her)* Don't count on me.

Emily: Why?

Mokai: I'm a stranger.

Emily: We are all strangers.

75

Mokai:	I'm a bird.
Emily:	Bird?
Mokai:	Birds have wings. Emily, I have wings.
Emily:	You... *(Brightens up)* O' I get you. I've got wings too... To fly after you, if that is what you mean.
Mokai:	*(Pulls her close)* You will fly after me! To where?
Emily:	Anywhere. Wherever!
Mokai:	*(Trance-like)* Not to the Savannah. The little cottage is no more.
Emily:	What?
Mokai:	The rains; the storm; the tornado! *(Stares at Emily)* That's why I've got the wings.
Emily:	*(Laughs softly)* You've got the wings! Sounds like the Pastor.
	(Sings in monotone)
	I got a wing, you got a wing.
	All God's children got a wing;
	When I get to Heaven
	I'm gonna put on my wing
	And shout all over God's Heaven.
	Heaven! Heaven!
	Everybody talking about Heaven,
	ain't going there, Heaven!
	Heaven! Heaven!
Mokai:	*(Enchanted)* I like that.
Emily:	It's the Pastor's song whenever he is happy.
Mokai:	*(Excited)* Never mind Pastor. *(He takes her hand)* ... To the river... Sing!
	(Hop, dance round stage arm in arm, singing)
	(Emily sings. Mokai tries to join in. Enter Iya'jo)
Iya'jo:	*(From off stage)* Glory be. The Meek One of the Lord...
Mokai:	Glory be.

76

(Emily jumps clear of Mokai)

Iya'jo: Over here. *(Beckons to Mokai who goes to meet her. Emily is by herself. Iya'jo, confidentially)*Good news. Pastor got Sisi Lagos off your back. She will never again tread the sand of Olifie. Ever!

Mokai: I know.

Iya'jo: Who told you? *(Iya'jo looks suspiciously at Emily)*

Emily: I'd better be going to the river.

(She goes. Iya'jo stares at her until exit)

Iya'jo: Go easy with her. Pastor hasn't got over Sisi Lagos incident.

Mokai: Sisi Lagos didn't do anything wrong.

Ija'jo: She did. She tried to ruin you for the sin of the flesh...

Mokai: I only helped her out.

Iya'jo: *(Exasperated)* You say that! You, the Meek One of the Lord!

Mokai: I gave all the money she gave me into the box of the Lord.

Iya'jo: *(Scandalised)* She gave you money! And you put sin money into the box of the Lord?

Mokai: I gave it all to the Pastor himself.

Iya'jo: Forgive, Lord! He did not know where the money came from. You must pray to avoid the wrath of the Pastor. He was just beginning to accept you, before Sisi Lagos started you on.

Mokai: Pastor said I have Belzeebub!

Iya'jo: *(Winks)* Don't worry about that. You'll learn more about Olifie as time goes on. *(Looking left and right)* You were running away from something, before the Lord sent you to Olifie, weren't you?

Mokai: They were after me... But my inner power saw

77

me through... *(Getting emotional)* O' too many things, too many things had happened in the past...

Iya'jo: We know... The devils were after you... But the Lord beat them to it. That's now in the past.

(Mokai nods)

You have to forget the past... Emily is a rising lamb of Olifie. Now you make it two. *(Maternally)* The Meek One of the Lord. Glory be... *(Smiling)* Go now; go see Emily to the river... go...

Iya'jo watches Mokai disappear with maternal joy. Mokai suddenly stops. Slow chanting from afar. Emily rushes past Mokai with empty water pot, out of breath. Emily and Iya'jo are grouping together when three men appear, creeping slowly in with deadly menace. One carries a roll of lasso rope, the rest clubs and charms. They are cultmen from Akilagun in various cult loin-cloths and tops. The leader wears elaborate head-dress. The leader points his wand towards Mokai. Like a mine detector. He nods with satisfaction.

Leader: *(To the rest)* It's him alright.,. Eh stranger! Greetings from the top of the hill that has no base.

(He bows and beckons Mokai to come over. Mokai refuses)

Iya'jo: *(Very frightened, backs up pulling Emily with her)* Pastor!... Master of Olifie!

(They run off). Mokai has now been surrounded by the three men. They are stalking Mokai)

Leader: *(Bows)* The High Priest is no more. The Oracle points to you. The reason is not for us to ask. You are the chosen one. The Council want you back.

Mokai: No... No...

Leader: You're coming back with us.

78

	(He is waving his charm in front of Mokai, as Pastor leads the others in, ringing bell vigorously. The Cultmen stop and assemble together. Mokai seems immobile in the centre of the two parties)
Pastor:	What seek ye, intruders?
Cultmen:	We are no intruders. We come to take our own. (Their leader points his staff at Mokai) Him!
Pastor:	You will take no-one from here; so depart in peace.
Leader:	Stranger, we do not come to disturb your peace. We have journeyed through rivers and mountains in search of our man. The Elders await us. The entire community awaits the results of our mission. He must come with us.
Pastor:	We have no time for bantering. Our service must begin soon. You must depart.
Leader:	(Stubbornly) We cannot go back without a result. We are prepared to negotiate to have our man... For instance, that lady over there bears the aura of a mother of earth from our side.
	(Iya'jo gasps in consternation and grabs Pastor's dress apparently for protection)
	We shall do nothing about that. He is all we want.
Pastor:	Your tongue of Babel does not blend in our ears; for the man you seek arrived here in search of peace. He is now the Meek One of the Lord. A servant true to his mercies... So.
	(Unintelligible murmur of dissent from the Cultmen)
Leader:	(Affronted) Meek One of the Lord! (Contemptuously) Servant! No... that cannot be so. (Desperately) I appeal to you in the name of whatever you believe! Give us back our Priest!
	(Consternation amongst flock)
Pastor:	You mean your heathen Priesthood?

79

Leader:	*(Forced to reveal)* The only hope according to the Oracle.
Pastor:	He has found peace in Olifie.
Leader:	Olifie... what is Olifie? *(Turns to men)* Was this not the former site of Ijomu, the village of two hills?
Cultmen:	*(Severally)* Yes, yes... It has been for generations.
Pastor:	That is no more. It is Olifie... Olifie for ever...
Flock:	Halleluia!
Leader:	*(Attacking)* Quaint names of quaint rituals is no concern of ours. We say let the garden bloom with a thousand species of roses. All we are here for is our man *(indicates Mokai)* whose past is our future. Allow him to make a choice.
	(Negative reactions from the flock)
Pastor:	You carry the past around with you. Right. *(To Mokai)* The heathens have brought the past back to you. Now, the Meek One of the Lord, will you step back into the past, or will you choose Olifie?
Mokai:	You said I have Belzeebub!
	(Flock is shocked)
Pastor:	*(Embarrassed, but quickly recovers)* We'll discuss that later.
Mokai:	... And the Lord's Supper!
Pastor:	*(Unruffled this time)* That's with the Lord.
Leader:	*(Takes advantage of the situation. Calls out in monotone pointing his staff at Mokai. Incantation)*
	Come, come home
	Agbe kii kú si ilu idáró *Agbe never dies in the town of Dyeing.*
Cultmen:	*(Together)* Come home.

Leader:	**Alukò kii kú si ilú ikosùn**	*Aluko never dies in town of osun*
Men:	Come, come home.	
Leader:	**Lékeléke kii kú si ilu ikefun**	*Lekeleke never dies in the town of chalk.*
Cultmen:	Come, come home.	
Leader:	**Odideré ò gbodò kú s'óko iwáje**	*Parrot never dies searching for food*
Cultmen:	Come, come home.	

(Mokai is responding, albeit involuntarily to the Cultmen's appeal. Leader holds a small calabash aloft tauntingly towards Mokai)

Leader: Here is the effigy of your mate
The placenta that kept you company
On your journey to this earth.
You met to part...
You part to meet... *(Tantalising)*
It's here!

(Mokai is moving, sleep-walking towards Cultmen)

Pastor: *(Shouts desperately)* The Meek One of the Lord!

(Mokai stops)

Flock: *(Together)* The Meek One of the Lord!

Leader / C.Men: *(Continues)* Come, come home.

Iya'jo: *(Comes forward desperately)* Stop!

(All stop. Iya'jo ties her robe between her thighs showing most of them. She stands feet apart and hits the frontal part of her waist and declaims)

Children of Woman, Kirgina is your passage into the world. Any of you have other passage? *(Silence)* And who taught a child to call 'Mother'?

Leader: *(To his men)* She is the mother of Earth, I said it. *(To Iya'jo formally)* Since when did you ever see mother-snake and her children on stroll?

81

(Iya'jo is lost for a second)

You see... you are wide off the mark. No witch is tough enough to bite off her own clitoris.

Cultmen: E è wo! Taboo!!! No! No witch can...

Iya'jo: *(Walking up to Mokai)* But the snake is still the bearer of her children. What other name do you want to give to mother? When is a mother not a mother? *(Leader is lost)*

(Forcefully to Mokai)

You, son of woman
Placenta is your mate.
You both belong to mother *(Opening her legs)*
Come, make your journey a second time!
Come for rebirth... Pass through...   *(She shouts)*
Pass! Pass! Pass! Etc, etc).

(Mokai crawls through Iya'jo's legs. Cultmen express despair. Pastor and flock are lost as Mokai comes out closer to the flock, feeling confident)

Iya'jo: *(Wildly triumphant)* You've lost. Now go!

Leader: You are Mother of Earth alright. But you are out of touch... very much out of touch. *(He signals to his followers and starts to incantate)*

Gbégbé kiìgbé s'óko
Àyúnbò lowo y'enu
Atelesè won a bè'nà wò.

Cultmen: (Chant):	Ewon le mu fawon o, ewon	Drag you home
	Árá o rè gbárrá.	With chains
	Ewon la mu fà wón o, ewón	We shall drag you home.

Leader: Árá o è gbájù u 'o

Cultmen: *(Chorus)* Ewòn la mú fà won o, èwòn.

82

<table>
<tr><td></td><td>(Cultman carrying the rope suddenly throws it and catches Mokai in lasso. Cultmen pull as they sing in rhythm)</td></tr>
<tr><td>Leader:</td><td>Emi la mú fà wón o?</td></tr>
<tr><td>Cultmen:</td><td>(Chorus) Ewon la mu fà wón o, ewón.</td></tr>
</table>

(Mokai struggles as he is being pulled away. Pastor seems perplexed)

Iya'jo: *(Appealing to Pastor)* They've got us... Pastor do something... You've got to stop them...

(Pastor is befogged as Cultmen chant triumphantly, pulling Mokai with ease.

The power of Olifie!... Pastor invoke it...

(Pastor wakes up. Pulls out his huge cross to Mokai appealing. Mokai grabs the cross. Iya'jo grabs round his waist. The flock forms a tug of war team and starts to pull. Pastor is saying holy words. 'Jah! Jah! Jah!' Etc. Flock is shouting 'Holy! Holy! Holy!' Etc. Cultmen and leader are chanting as they pull. Mokai is being pulled a few feet each way. At last, the Cultmen seem to be gaining ground when suddenly we hear a loud report of gunfire. The combatants are shocked to a standstill. For a few moments, another burst of automatic gunfire, which sounds nearer than the first)

Leader: What is that?

Pastor: *(On the mark)* They have arrived... Our Army of Heaven have arrived... Halleluia...

Flock: *(Taking cue)* Halleluia!!!

(Cult leader is panic stricken as more gunfire reports come nearer... His men also panic)

Pastor: *(Leads and Flock sings)* 'Onward Christian Soldiers'.

(Cultmen undo rope and flee in disorder. The

Flock are dancing and singing 'Onward Christian Soldiers', and clapping with shouts of Halleluia. Holy, Holy, Holy. They are getting possessed... A slow blackout)

OLIFIE

(GIRLS / MOKAI)

(Lights up. Two girls, Derin and Titi are on stage)

(Same part of Olifie. They are expecting someone. Derin is the more active while Titi is rather calm)

Titi:	*(Anxious)* Do you think he will come?
Derin:	Oh yes. He must pass this way to the river.
Titi:	I don't think I can wait any longer
Derin:	What's the hurry? You want fun or not?
Titi:	But how are we going to put it to him?
Derin:	We just ask him. Same way as Sisi Eko did.

(She demonstrates wiggling with exaggeratedly coquettish voice, meant to be seductive)

Eh Mokai! Eh... eh... The Meek One of the Lord... Let's see some part of you eh!

(The two girls laugh)

Titi:	*(Adventurous)* I'll ask him. *(She tries to imitate Derin poorly. She admits failure)* No... I can't. You'd better do it.
Derin:	And then she'd say 'Mokai' Super Jee... Super Jee!
Titi:	What does that mean?
Derin:	Who knows. But he likes it.
Titi:	I still can't believe it.
Derin:	You don't believe me? Wait till you see Uzo.
Titi:	Was she there too?
Derin:	No. I told her.

84

Titi:	Did you tell Uzo about this meeting?
Derin:	I did, but I don't think she will come.
Titi:	Let's go call her... The more, the merrier.
Derin:	No, We'll miss Mokai. Let's wait here.
Titi:	I'm frightened about the whole thing. I think it's dangerous.
Derin:	What's dangerous about it?
	(She has no answer)
Titi:	And Emily? Supposing she gets to know of our game?
Derin:	Emily can go nut for all I care. What's she to him?
Titi:	*(Admiring touch line)* Dee for Derin!
Derin:	All that rolling on the floor and grabbing Mokai's legs doesn't impress me...
Titi:	Dee for Dee!
Derin:	You'll see. The next vigil I'll beat her to it. You know. I could roll and shout and tear off my clothes before grabbing Pastor himself. Watch me!
Titi:	Don't do that! He might find you out.
Derin:	Fun is fun. Emily's nonsense about Holy Union doesn't work with me, you know.
Titi:	You are so matter-of-fact.
	(They hear movement off stage. Titi jumps. They wait, but no-one enters)
	(Nervous) I don't know why, but I feel nervous. Feel my heart-beat.
	(Pushes her chest towards Derin. She gently cups her and over Titi's breast, caresses it a bit and then squeezes it hard. Titi jerks and yells)
	Devil...
	(They both giggle. Someone approaches. They

85

both smarten up, expecting Mokai. But it is Uzo who comes in a hurry)

Uzo!

Uzo.	Glory be.
Titi:	Glory be. Uzo!
Derin:	You make it. Did you see him...!
Uzo:	Shh! He'll be here any minute. He's tidying up the vestry. Is it all according to plan?
Derin:	Of course. Get your money ready, everyone. 'Church due' Sisi Eko called it. *(Giggles)*
Titi:	*(Worried)* Emily trusts me.
Derin:	She trusts me too.
Uzo:	She is out of the way.
Titi:	Where is she?
Uzo:	At the river. *(Smiling maliciously)* She asked me not long ago if I saw Mokai. My brain just clicked fast and I said... 'On the way to the river'. And off she ran – after him.

(They laugh)

Titi:	But she might be back in a moment if she doesn't find him there.
Derin:	*(Furious)* What's this nonsense about Emily? You better go and leave us to get on with it.
Titi:	*(Offended)* You can say that now that you see Uzo.
Derin:	You kept on as if we are planning something awful.
Uzo:	What's the quarrel about now? The man does as he pleases; he may not even stop to talk to us...
Titi:	Alright, I'm sorry. But you will ask him first?
Uzo:	I'll stop him.

86

Derin:	I'll do the talking... *(Remembering)* O'yes, we'll have to sing his song first...
Titi:	What song?
Uzo:	I know it.
Derin:	And I know it too. You just hum along with us.
Titi:	Shh!

(Mokai approaches humming "Onward Christian Soldiers". The girls freeze. They organise themselves in position. Mokai enters)

Uzo:	*(With nervous courage)* Greetings. The Meek One of the Lord.
Mokai:	Glory be little lambs.
All:	Glory be.

(They look at one aother for the next step)

Derin:	*(Bold-faced)* Where're you going now?
Mokai:	To the river.
Uzo:	*(Teasing)* No Belzeebub?
Mokai:	*(Good-naturedly)* No. Belzeebub.
Uzo:	And the Lord's Supper?
Mokai:	*(Smiling)* It's with the Lord.

(The girls giggle. Awkward silence. Mokai is about to go)

Derin:	*(Bravado)* Mokai Super Jee!

(Mokai is stunned. He stares hard at Derin. Incredulously, Derin repeats)

Mokai Super Jee.

(Mokai shakes his head and laughs quietly)

Uzo:	*(Butts in)* Mokai Super Jee!
Titi:	*(Trembling voice)* Mokai Super Jee.
All:	*(Severally)* Mokai Super Jee!
Mokai:	Who taught you that?

Derin:	**We know.**
Uzo:	*(Blatant)* Sisi Eko knows too.
Derin:	We saw it all.
Mokai:	What do you want?
	(Silence)
Derin:	The same. Fun.
Uzo:	And we have the 'Church due' ready.
	(She jingles some coins for Mokai's benefit)
Mokai:	*(Thinks)* You better get along to the village.
Derin:	*(Steps forward to demonstrate towards Mokai)* "Mokai, Super Jee, let's see some of you".
The Rest:	Yes... yes... C'mon...
Mokai:	Not with you little lambs.
Uzo:	*(Drops the coins near Mokai. Others do the same)* It's all for you... And the song. We can sing it too.
Mokai:	Right then. *(Picks up coins)* This is for the **Lord's Box**... Sing... the song now...
All:	Mokai a, Sommori O Mokai, the veritable playboy.
	Aiye ni gbà O Keep rolling on;
	Ilé aiyé nse be e ni i Whatever happens,
	Ko ni tu o... Life'll still go on.

(Mokai repeats song with girls. He takes out a crucifix tied to waist and starts to swing it up and down gradually with a good-natured threat at the girls. Mokai stops laughing as he puts the crucifix back)

Derin.	Now for the real thing.
Uzo:	Yes, the real thing!
Mokai:	To help you out?
All:	*(Mindless of what he means)* Yes... yes... now.
Derin:	*(Repeats demonstration)* Mokai Super Jee, let's see some of you,..

88

Mokai:	*(Thinking they have no more money left)* **More for the box of the Lord then.**
Uzo:	That's all we have.
Mokai:	That's it.
Derin:	You know we never have any money.
Uzo:	We have to find the one we gave you.
Mokai:	No way... I'm off to the river...
Titi:	*(Suddenly)* I have more... here...
	(The rest are surprised as Titi brings out more money for Mokai)
	Take it all.
Mokai:	*(He is now beaten. Nevertheless he takes the money as extra booty)* **Good, But it still has to be later... See you all later...**
All:	Now, now...
	(He goes . They stand in his way)
Mokai:	I said later.
Derin:	No... that's cheating.
Uzo:	That's not right...
Titi:	You have got all I have... **not right...**
Derin:	Give us back our money.
Uzo:	Or we'll tell Pastor about you.
	(They bar his way)
Mokai:	All this money goes to him. Get off, I've got to get to the river...
	(They push against him)
	C'mon little lambs...
Titi:	*(Ferocious)* I'm no little lamb. Give me back my money.
All:	Give it back.

89

	(They pull at his clothes and get nasty. He gets worked up and turns on them)
Mokai:	Alright, you ply the river bed too far; you will meet Olueri, stormy god of the river.
	(He jumps, making frightening sound that sends them scattering with fright)
	Wayah!
	(He chases after them ferociously as they back away from him. He pursues them helter-skelter off-stage. They yell and shout, making noise off-stage. Uzo runs on stage from opposite direction. Then, Derin panting. But Titi continues struggling and yelling off-stage against Mokai)
Derin:	Titi fell... he's got her... I saw him...
Uzo:	He's beating her?
Derin:	I don't know.
	(Titi is shouting 'Help. Oh! Help, Oh! Etc. off-stage)
Uzo:	*(Shouts)* Leave her alone!
Derin:	*(Panicking)* He'll kill her... Help... Murder... Help...
	(Then silence comes over the whole place off-stage and on. The girls, fearing the worst, are confused and undecided).
Uzo:	*(Lamenting)* What are we going to do?
Derin:	Pastor will be here any minute.
Uzo:	*(Backing out)* I didn't want to get involved. You came for me.
Derin:	You came by yourself. You went searching for him... all over didn't you?
Uzo:	*(Beaten)* O' what's happening to Titi now?
Derin:	*(Guiltily shouting)* Don't ask me... You told me that he was in the vestry and Titi gave him more

90

	money. She said she had little money. Then suddenly she gave him all. Everything she had, and now... *(Perplexed)*
Uzo/Derin:	*(Holler)* Titi!
	(Enter Pastor, Iya'jo)
Pastor:	*(Stretching his hands out)* Little Lambs of Olifie!
Uzo:	*(Petrified)* Super Jee got her!
Pastor:	*(Irritated)* Super Jee?
Derin:	We were minding our own business, when he began to chase us.
Pastor:	Who chased you?
Uzo:	*(Realising she has not said the right name)* It's Mokai.
Pastor:	*(Collapses into himself)* No!
Uzo:	He's got Titi. She fell off in the new cemetery.
Iya'jo:	In the cemetery?
Pastor:	He keeps calling himself Mokai... Well Mokai he shall be. *(Yells)* Mokai! Mokai!
	(Enter Titi dishevelled and thoroughly shaken. She doubles in. She tries to smarten up. Pastor takes her in his arms. She is incoherent)
Pastor:	*(Comforting her)* Little lamb...
Iya'jo:	Speak child...
Derin:	*(Butts in)* He chased us...
Uzo:	Yes he did...
Pastor:	Quiet you two... *(Tenderly to Titi)* Now little lamb, what happened?
Titi:	He chased us... I fell on Papa Abel's grave then... he chased me... I fought him hard. But he... he *(she is collapsing)*
Pastor:	Elohi! *(Rushes towards exit and hollers at the top of his voice)* Mokai!!! *(Agitated, turns towards Iya'jo)* I want to see his face: now!

91

Iya'jo:	*(Gestures for peace)* I will talk with the girl. *(Takes Titi aside)*
Pastor:	*(Infuriated)* No, no. Enough of whispering in Olifie. I have warned you about him. You whisper: you play it down. First it was Sisi Eko. You didn't believe it until you actually saw him running amock in the vestry... with the woman's headtie around his waist!
Iya'jo:	Peace, Pastor.
Pastor:	Then Emily... and now he is chasing fresh innocent lambs around the sacred homes of the dead, calling himself *(To girls)* what again?
Derin / Uzo:	*(Together)* Super Jee!
Pastor:	You hear that?
	(Enter Mokai in a hurry. He is about to make for another exit)
Iya'jo:	*(Trying to stop him)* Here he is. The Meek One of the Lord. Come here.
Pastor:	Not that.
Mokai:	*(Slows down)* Got to wash down in the river. *(He bows reverently as he goes)* Glory be.
Pastor:	Stop...
	(Mokai has gone. Pastor turns to Iya'jo)
	See that! Now, see that. He's guilty as sin.
Iya'jo:	He must come back to tell his side of the matter.
Pastor:	He's got too many sides already. *(Finally)* I don't want to set my eyes on him again.
Iya'jo:	Patience, Pastor.
Pastor:	*(To girls)* Get you all into the vestry for a session of absolution. Your fasting has begun.
	(Exit girls)
	(Accusingly to Iya'jo) You promised to take charge of him when I decided to throw him out the day

after Pentecost.

Iya'jo: Time... Pastor!

Pastor: Time? Olifie was love and tranquility before he showed his face here. Since then what? I exorcised him. He fasted. With the privilege of communicating with the dead. I elected him the Meek One of the Lord... Then what?

Iya'jo: I'm trying my best. Must be his people... One never knows what they did to him before....

Pastor: *(Ignoring Iya'jo's statement)* Right under your nose, he turned Emily into a two-face within the flock. You promised to investigate the matter. Where is the report?... None! *(He remembers Emily)*... Emily! Where is Emily?

Iya'jo: She's gone to the river.

Pastor: No! Not to the river!

Iya'jo: So the girls said.

Pastor: And he's gone there too! *(Works himself into a fit)* Why? Why? *(Stretches up his arms)* Elohi! Elohi! Lama! Sabaktaaani!

Iya'jo: *(Holding him)* Peace, Master. Peace.

Pastor: *(Cursing)* Know this. If even the sky is left with one solitary star, Mokai shall never enter the Kingdom of Heaven!

Iya'jo: *(Pleading)* Mercy, whither will you drive the sinner?

Pastor: To his people!

Iya'jo: No. Not to them! The same that came for him with rope of magic?

Pastor: Yes! Them!

Iya'jo: Master you will not do that. Is he not the same that prophesied great events on Olifie?

93

Pastor:	I want none of his great events on Olifie *(Deadly cool, with long pause as he peers into Iya'jo)* And you! What do you know, daughter!
Iya'jo:	*(Intensely)* The teaching of the Lord.
Pastor:	Forget the catechism: what do you know about the wind of confusion. The evil vibrations that ravage Olifie?
Iya'jo:	*(Confounded)* Me?
Pastor:	*(Accusing)* Those heathens called you Mother of Earth. You said nothing.
Iya'jo:	What was I to say?
Pastor:	You joined them. You gave a performance that was strange and weird in the eyes of the Lord...
Iyajo:	*(Confused)* I... I... only answered fire with fire...
Pastor:	*(Grips her and shouts to her face)* You have other fire beside the fire of the Lord! What is Mother of Earth?
	(Iya'jo is too petrified to speak)
Pastor:	*(Fiercely)* What is Mother of Earth!
Iya'jo:	No... no... I'm not Mother of Earth. It's them. They are their fathers' children. *(Vigorously)* I never attended any meeting of the large birds of the night... Oh the thought of it... Akilagun is behind me. I thought the past is gone for ever. I thought I will be left alone — in Peace.
Pastor:	Speak, daughter!
Iya'jo:	*(Panting. Disjointed but coherent)* Part of me has gone for ever... I never saw it. I never touched it... The old Wizard wouldn't let me... But I heard the wailing... thin and loud. The Ancestors. They made me carrier of their child. Mother saw it. *(Declaims)* The Child of the Ancestors does not belong to me!
Pastor:	*(Quite confused)* Babel! Tongue of Babel!

94

Iya'jo:	That was the order of the Old Wizard of the Little Cottage at the Edge of the Savannah!
Pastor:	More Babel... *(Stern)* You shall speak in the tongue of the Lord!
Iya'jo:	*(Plaintively)* Yes. I will. It started on the eve of the arrival of the Ancestors. At Akilagun. I was deceived by the sun... and the rainbow... on the hill. A mere child I was on my way back from the river... on the eve of the festival of the Ancestors. It was bright with bits of drizzle. I had emerged from the home forest on the last hill. I saw rainbow arched beyond the village. I had time, I thought: I stood to watch... to make wishes of fortune. Then the rainbow went: the drizzling stopped. And the sun came back, all red. Then it began to change into all colours. I watched some more. But without warning, the sun went and darkness began to creep in. I held on to my water pot; and hurried on through the pits and gravels on the path. Water was splashing all over me when the voice came from the bush... "Welcome, bride of the ancestors..." The ancestors!!! the bush... "Welcome, bride of the ancestors..." The ancestors.!!!

(Light fades out on Pastor and Iya'jo, and fades in. Flash-back in colour lighting. We see a young girl carrying a water pot on her head, miming hurry. She looks left and right in fear. Drum rolls and a man in mask jumps in her path. Then another, and another until they are six. Each man dangles a piece of fifteen-inch bamboo held in front of their mid-rift, threateningly towards her; simulating sexual dancing orgy. They encircle her menacingly. She is stopped in whichever direction she tries to run. They close in on her, one takes her pot. Then a long drum roll introduces a seventh with the most elaborate and grotesque

mask of all. He dances menacingly to the group and mimes an order. She pleads. She is exhausted and flops down. He briefly engages her. She is rolling as they encircle her; engaging her attention one by one. After a while the leader gives the order: They carry the girl away struggling while the leader dances behind them until exit with the drum rolling. Flute. They continue to dance, using their bamboo suggestively all over the stage. They exit.

Light fades in on Pastor and Iya'jo as they were. But now Pastor is holding Iya'jo who is numb with exhaustion and grief. As lights come on, Pastor is backing away from Iya'jo, who is sprawling and crawling towards Pastor. His mouth is ajar, his face full of terror and repulsion)

Pastor:	*(Barely audible)* Heathens! Heathens!
Iya'jo:	Help me. Don't move away...Master, stay...

(Pastor stops, transfixed)

Nobody believed me. Mother took me to the hermit in his little cottage... there the Old Wizard saw it... as it happened. He saw all seven creatures in his divination... before he took the baby... *(Gasps)* ... then... then...

Pastor:	That's alright for now...
Iya'jo:	... Then he put me through the rituals of the large Birds of the Night! ... But I never wanted it.
Pastor:	*(Thoroughly perplexed)* Peace, daughter, Peace!
Iya'jo:	I had none. No peace at Akilagun. The ancestors started me with a crowd. Then the rest... they came... crowd... farmers... hunters... carvers... cultmen... I didn't want the Secret of the Cult. They gave it to me... They plucked my plume; they ran my blade blunt... and the Wizard took the child... But I never attended the meeting. I never

wanted the power of the Mother of Earth...
Help... Pastor. It's them...

Pastor: *(Shakes her vigorously)* Halleluia... Halleluia... Lord... Lord... Lord... *(He rises in ecstasy and stretches his hands)* Your work is done!!!

Voice: *(Off-stage in a commanding tone)* Stay where you are!

Pastor: *(Taken aback. Freezes, then kneels expectantly)* Yes, Lord.

(Enter Lieutenant with his gun trained on the two)

Lieutenant: Don't move...

(Other soldiers enter one by one with their weapons, looking everywhere. One goes off-stage)

Pastor: *(Recovering his wit)* Peace be unto you.

Lieutenant: Never mind that. Seen any Army Officer around here?

Pastor: Army Officer?

Lieutenant: *(Impatient)* Don't repeat my question!

Pastor: *(Ruffled)* We see... no army officer around here.

Lieutenant: Sure?

Pastor: That's the truth!

Lieutenant: We have information that he headed this way.

Pastor: We know nothing about it.

Lieutenant: We don't want to hurt him.

Pastor: *(Unconvincingly)* I know.

Lieutenant: You don't know a thing. Where is he?

(A soldier brings in the flock. The girls are thoroughly frightened)

Soldier: I found them moaning and rolling on the floor, sir!

(He herds them with Iya'jo and Pastor)

97

Pastor:	*(Informing)* **They are sinners.**
Soldier:	**There is an old man clutching the bell chain. He won't move. Almost lifeless.**
Iya'jo:	**That's Papa Mose.**
Pastor:	**Our bell ringer.**
Lieutenant:	*(To soldier)* **He won't move?**
Soldier:	**I don't think he can, sir.**
Pastor:	**Ṭoo old. Ringing the bell is all he does.**
Lieutenant:	*(Making sure)* **You said you've seen no-one around, eh?**
Pastor:	*(Pleading)* **Truly we've seen no-one around. We are a simple flock of the Lord. And this place is Olifie.**
Lieutenant:	**Olifie?**
Pastor:	*(Getting confident)* **So pleases the Lord.**
Lieutenant:	*(Still suspicious)* **The Officer in question is our friend.**
Pastor:	*(Not convinced)* **I see... This here is the mother of the flock... Iya'jo...**
Iya'jo:	*(Promptly)* **We have seen no officer around here... *(Turns to flock)* Seen anyone?**
All:	**No.**
Lieutenant:	*(Looks around)* **This is all of you?**
Pastor:	**Members come and go in the service of the Lord. But we are all at the moment... that remain constant in his mercies.**
Lieutenant:	*(Checks with his men)* **Alright, we believe you. *(A bit relaxed)* Now you have to co-operate with us. There had been a little spot of bother in the capital, and we are trying to sort things out. Our friend headed this direction. That much we know. So keep your eyes open as loyal citizens and you shall be rewarded. 5000 American dollars.**

Think of it: foreign exchange. But we want him alive! Remember *(They are about to go, he stops, rather confidently)* if you see a group of rabbles in uniforms looking for same officer, say nothing. Nothing about us, nothing about the officer, right?

Pastor: *(Involuntarily)* Right.

(They exit. Their weapons pointing in all directions)

Iya'jo: *(Coming to)* What's happening?

Pastor: A spot of bother, he said.

Iya'jo: With those things in their hands!

Pastor: *(Goes in direction of the soldiers for a look. He comes back as he sees nothing much)* Now between us. Anybody seen any army officer around here or anywhere?

Iya'jo: Not me.

Others: *(Severally)* No, not me.

Pastor: Glory be.

Flock: Glory be.

Pastor: We all stick together. When they start like that you never know how they'll end.

Iya'jo: *(Concerned)* Emily... and... *(Cautiously)* Mokai.

Pastor: They are in the hands of the Lord... *(Declares)* Olifie is in the hands of the Lord. All cases of sinful acts and indiscipline are hereby suspended. Olifie is one again.

Flock: Halleluia!

(Enter Emily. Agitated and upset. She had apparently dodged the Lieutenant and his men. She collapses in Iya'jo's arms)

Emily: Soldiers!

Iya'jo: They were here.

99

Emily:	Not those. Another group. They've got Mokai. They're tearing him into pieces. They're killing him... They're... *(She is incoherent)*
	(Panic sets in among the Flock)
Pastor:	Nobody panics... Now Emily, calm down... tell us...
Emily:	We were by the riverside. I mean I was by the riverside, when a man appeared from the bush. He was all ragged. I thought he was a spirit of some dead soldier. I was about to run off, but Mokai went straight to him. They got talking about something. Then Mokai followed him behind the Iroko tree. After a while, Mokai came out in the man's ragged uniform. He began fooling around splashing water and shouting orders and laughing. That was when these other soldiers appeared from the bush. Mokai's friend took off in Mokai's cassock. They kept calling him to stop but he wouldn't. The next thing we saw him at the far end of river, scuttling across the timber bridge on his hands. They started shooting at him until he dropped into the river without a sound. Then Mokai made for the bush. But they flew at him and brought him down, and started punching him. He fought back, but they tumbled on him and butted him down. I begged and shouted, but they did not even notice me... until the little one started making some move, smiling and winking at me. I ran for it. He kept shouting at me to stop or he'll shoot. But he didn't shoot... he just stood there shouting and laughing. They are determined to kill Mokai... It's all my fault. *(Hysterical)* Forgive me... He didn't do anything wrong. I got him to the river... He didn't... *(A gunfire report. Emily screams)* They've done it. Forgive me, Mokai, forgive...
Pastor:	Stop, Emily! Stop.

100

(She calms down)

Listen everybody. Olifie is in a stage of siege...
We are invaded. But if the Lord is for us, who is
he that will turn his weapon against Olifie?

Iya'jo:	*(The rest echo Iya'jo)*
Pastor:	Fasting starts for all of us from this moment. Prayer is our power; and the Lord will see Olifie through this tribulation. *(Declaims)* Alpha and Omega!
Flock:	Holy! Holy! Holy!
Pastor:	You that saw Daniel out of the den of lions!
Flock:	Ho-ooo-ly!
Pastor:	Deliver Mokai.
Flock:	Amen!
Pastor:	Deliver Mokai! Deliver Mokai!
Flock:	Amen! Amen!
Pastor:	You that saw Jonah through the belly of the whale!
Flock:	Holy!
Pastor:	You that saw your Shadrach, Messhach and Abednego through the furnace of Nebukadnezzar!
Flock:	Holy!
Pastor:	You that saw your only son through all the temptations of Satan and his schemes.
Flock:	Holy! Holy! Holy!
Pastor:	Come down to us in this hour of tribulation in Olifie!
Flock:	Holy!
Pastor:	Ye armies of Heaven. Come down, come hither. Tarry hither and be with us.
Flock:	Holly!!!

101

Pastor:	*(Thoroughly worked up)*
	Now! I say now,
	Now, now, now... now!
	Jah! Jah!
	Kurajejitamah!!!
	Bulataki Ajagumolatabi!
	Et-Ofeti-Ludo-Ludo-Ludo
	Come down, come down
	Come down to
	O-L-I-F-I-E!!
Flock:	*(Ecstatically)* **Halleluia!!!**
	Halleluia!!!
	Halleluia!!!
Pastor/Flock:	*(All begin to sing)*
	"Onward Christian Soldiers..."

(At a point during the singing the earlier soldiers enter. Retreating with their back to the stage. One of them covers their entrance, while the rest face the Flock)

Lieutenant:	Listen all of you. The so-called Revolutionary Association of Tough Soldiers –RATS– have got General Baado. It is a do-or-die mission for us to rescue him. Now you'll do exactly as I say.
	(Cowed silence)
Pastor:	*(Bravely)* Our brother is involved.
Lieutenant:	*(Angry)* Shut up!
	(Dead silence)
	Now you'll stand where you are, and continue singing. Whatever happens, whosoever comes this way, you take no notice. Just sing on. Right?
	(Pastor nods uncertainly)
	(To Pastor) You.
Pastor:	Yes.
Lieutenant:	Keep your people in tight discipline. These rabbles call themselves Rats; we shall treat

102

them like rats. If you behave right, history will remember you. And you shall be rewarded. If not, ashes will be the remains of you all. I mean that. Any questions? *(He doesn't wait for an answer)* Right. *(To his men)* Take positions.

(The soldiers take various strategic positions of ambush. One is left behind to observe the entrance route. Meanwhile, Pastor has led the Flock into "Onward Christian Soldiers", this time with fear in flat monotone in contrast to earlier fervour. Fade out and fade in for time lapse.

The sentry finally signals the approach of the RATS. Enter the RATS. They anxiously cover their path with guns. Mokai is led in, tied with rope, with hood over his head. He falls and rises as he is pushed and shoved. He has been beaten drunk. He collapses and stays put.

Emily, who had hitherto resigned herself to the situation, screams)

Emily:	Mokai!!
Pastor:	*(Stops her from cutting loose)* Shut up!
RATS Leader:	Stop!

(Flock sings on raggedly, unnaturally, in confusion. RATS Leader is enraged)

I say quiet!

(Singing stops)

Have you no ears? Are you stones? You stand here singing like frogs while the nation bleeds its way to total revolution.

(Dead silence as the Flock is cowed once again)

Seen any soldiers lately?

Pastor:	No...
RATS Leader:	Not at all?
Pastor:	Not at all.

RATS Leader: *(Seems satisfied. Proclaims)* On behalf of the Supreme Council of the Revolutionary Association of Tough Soldiers, I declare this area an operational base, until further notice. Anybody who moves without permission will be shot. Yours is the privilege to see the conclusion of the struggle that began days ago in the capital. You shall tell your children's children that you were the first to witness the capture, and execution, of the only pillar of the old order left at large. *(Announcing)* You are face to face with General Finto Asantiko Baado!

(Mokai grunts protests feebly. He is butted and pulled. Emily runs screaming towards Mokai. The RATS open fire on her. She falls close to Mokai in a hail of bullets. The soldiers in ambush also open fire. All the RATS are mowed down, leader first. There is chaos and confusion as the Flock try to run away in disorder. Iya'jo braves it, she half carries, half drags Emily. The victorious soldiers are shouting.

Pastor also examines Emily. Shakes head in doubt, but optimistic nonetheless)

Lieutenant: *(Exclaims)* She'll live. *(Incensed and untying Mokai)* Long live General Baado! Long live the Reformation.

Soldiers: *(Severally)*
Death to the Rats.
Death to all Revolutionaries.
Long live General Baado.
Long live the Reformation.
Long live the Nation.
Hurrah!

(They shoot wildly into the air with sound of triumph, as... Slow Blackout.
Lights come up slowly. Mokai is seated on a chair

LC. He is supported on all sides to prevent him from falling. He is half-conscious. Two Reformation Soldiers stand guard by him. The others parade up and down apprehensively with their weapons. Pastor and Flock are kneeling CR. Paying obeisance to Mokai, as ordered by the Soldiers. Lieutenant conducts with his swagger stick and the others respond mechanically)

Pastor: Hail! Hail! Hail!
We pledge our support for thee.

Flock: Long live the Nation,
Long live the Reformation,
Long live General Finto,
Asantiko Baado.

(This is being repeated several times. It is obvious that the Lieutenant is anxiously expecting callers. At last the sentry signals the arrival of the visitors. Lieutenant makes sure that everyone is alert. The chanting is made more lively. Enter Major Ndem, a civilian personage, Professor Tomwuruwuru, henceforth referred to as Ndem and TWW respectively. They are accompanied by guards and assistants carrying weapons and medical kits).

Lieutenant: *(Rudely to Flock)* Alright, that'll do. Get off your knees... C'mon...

(Pastor and Flock are almost flat out. Iya'jo is completely bewildered. Lieutenant turns to his men)

Attention!

(They click their heels in salutation. Mokai stirs a bit)

(Formally) Sir! So glad you are here, Sir!

(to Ndem)

(Ndem nods approval. He marches briskly to Mokai and salutes)

105

Ndem:	Major Ndem sir, with message of regret, anger and congratulation from the Supreme Military Council of the Reformation, Sir!
Mokai:	*(Deliriously)* Emily... Emily?
Ndem:	Who sir?
	(Lieutenant makes 'Take no Notice' sign to Ndem)
Iya'jo:	O' poor kid...
	(Pastor jerks her to an abrupt silence)
Lieutenant:	*(Aside)* The RATS really committed some major crimes on his person before he was rescued, sir.
Ndem:	We got the picture from your dispatch. I have here with me Professor Tomwuruwuru, topmost of the Nation's specialists in medical science and a renowned consultant in International Affairs. He is for the cause.
TWW:	*(Beams pompously as he bows)* Simply call me 'Prof'!
Lieutenant:	Hello Prof? *(Handshakes)*
Mokai:	They got him. The rabbit on the log... then in the river... Where is she... Emily? *(Mutters unintelligibly)* I'm not me... Who's me?
Lieutenant:	*(To Mokai)* Everything will be alright sir. *(Aside to Ndem and TWW)* A bit of delirium, sir.
TWW:	*(Supremely confident)* I'll take care of that in a jiffy. (*He opens his box and takes out bottles and things. He examines Mokai)*
Ndem:	Good. The Proclamation! *(He reads from a scroll)* "Be it known to all Citizens of our Nation that the Supreme Military council of the Reformation ... (*He scans through lengthy passages)* Blah blah blah. After due consideration of the existing state of emergency in these dark hours in the life of our Nation — blah blah blah — Hereby, in the name of the said Council, hand

over all matters concerning the Nation, its citizens, its wealth, and all powers to manage same, to the august person of the gallant hero of our nation as Head of State, Supreme Commander of the Armed Forces, same being our Great Leader, General Finto Asantiko Baado!

All: *(Led by the Lieutenant)*

Long live the Nation

Long live the Reformation

Long live General Finto

Asantiko Baado!

Flock: *(Continuing mechanically)* Hail! Hail! Hail!

Lieutenant: Alright! Alright, that'll do... that'll do.

(TWW produces some strange stethoscope. He examines Mokai all over)

TWW: How do you feel, sir?

Mokai: *(Protests inaudibly)* Hm... hm... no, not me... no... no...

TWW: Beg your pardon, sir?

Mokai: *(Slurs)* I'm Mokai.

TWW: *(To others)* What is he saying?

Lieutenant: *(Confidentially)* Delirium. He doesn't remember much since the deadly assault, sir.

TWW: He can't remember a thing?

Ndem: *(Rather impatient)* We got that too in the dispatch. Something has to be done immediately. We have no time.

TWW: *(Still examining with his strange stethoscope. Feeling Mokai with fingers)* Leave it to me, Major... How exactly do you feel, sir?

Mokai: *(Protests feebly, unintelligibly)* Mmm... hm... no... no... Not me, not me... I'm Mokai.

TWW: Beg your pardon, sir?

107

(Lieutenant continues his 'Take no Notice' sign despairingly)

Ndem: *(To TWW)* How bad is it?

TWW: I'll soon find out. *(To Lieutenant)* You say he can't remember a thing?

Ndem: *(Impatiently)* Forget what he can't remember. Just treat him, Professor.

TWW: Alright, alright. We've got to make sure. *(Speaking to himself, he picks out an abominably huge syringe gingerly)* He can't remember a thing... That leaves us with the possibility of a complication... Amnesiamatra due to a severe injury to the region close to his vertebrae and...

Ndem: *(Interrupts him)* Think we can move him?

TWW: Not right away. He is suffering from terrible *shock for a start. (He mixes liquids)* Then there is the probability of rifle butts interference with the casing of the cerebrum. If that is so, he's survived a chance in a million. That's in keeping with most great men.

          (Pours more liquids and powder into a large container and stirs)

Ndem: That bad, eh?

TWW: *(Oblivious of Ndem's questions. Half to himself)* We've got to cool him down first.

          (Sucks concoction into syringe. Ndem looks uneasily on)

Ndem: *(Looking desperate)* It is very very serious then.

TWW: Nothing is ever 'very very serious' in the realm of medical science, Major.

          (Prepares Mokai for a jab. Ndem is restless at the proceedings)

          Here we go. The best of British apothecary.

TWW:	*(Macabre humour)* To the health of His Excellency!
	(Motions two men to close in. Feels Mokai's neck, then injects. Mokai yells and gives a struggle. The two men holding him hold him down. He is shaking with the syringe still in him. TWW is taking all the time...)
Mokai:	*(Shaking violently)* No... no... please let me go... no...
	(TWW nods with satisfaction)
Iya'jo:	*(Whose presence has all the while been forgotten with the others)* Poor kid... poor kid...
Lieutenant:	Shut up! Get off! *(Sternly to Pastor)* You're in charge of your people or are you not?
Pastor:	Sorry about that... C'mon Iya'jo. *(He murmurs some kind words to her. He comes back to watch in wonderment)*
Ndem:	*(Impatiently)* Go... go somewhere all of you!
	(Exeunt Flock)
Lieutenant:	*(Stops Pastor)* I suggest he stays sir... He has his uses sir...
	(Ndem frowns)
	Good reason, sir.
Ndem:	Ok... Him alone.
	(TWW is busy feeling Mokai with some meter reading object. He jots down points in notebook, murmuring medical jargon to himself. He watches with satisfaction as Mokai calms down a bit. Then he puts the object at the back of Mokai's waist)
TWW:	The General has been engaged in series of strenuous physical action prior to the attack. *(Gestures for absolute silence, quietly)* How did it all happen, sir?

	(All wait anxiously as Mokai murmurs)
Mokai:	*(Feebly)* They shot him... where's she... The river... in the river... *(He calms down, almost limp)*
TWW:	*(To Ndem uncertainly)* Probably his aide or something?

(Ndem gestures ignorance. TWW takes out a large bottle of red liquid and dips in the syringe)

It's more serious than I thought.

Ndem: Another one?

TWW: *(Nods)* This'll prepare him. Real American medical wizardry.

(Ndem is impressed)

Especially prepared for rejuvenating ageing rhinoceros down the Mississippi.

Ndem: *(Greatly impressed)* In America?

TWW: *(Nods)* Every cell in him will shoot out times over. You'll see.

(He injects another side of Mokai's neck. Mokai yells and grunts heavily. But without prolonged struggle. And he is twisting in rhythm. TWW seems satisfied)

We are getting there! Now the next step.

(He takes out a gadget that looks like a home made space headgear, with wires dangling from it. He dusts and adjusts it. Noticing the looks of horror on Ndem's face, he tries to reassure him)

TWW: This is the latest invention of Obolenvsky himself.

Ndem: Who?

TWW: *(Adjusting headgear)* Obolenvsky... The great Russian inventor... Ivanovitch Obolenvsky. *(Joking)* *(Ndem peers at the object)* But the label is American all the same. Here we go. *(He is fitting it on Mokai's head ceremoniously.*

110

He screws on the nuts and adjusts for size) A little large. Only fifty of them in circulation: and none of them for public sales. *(He finds a screw missing)* Where is the screw for this end? Damn it! *(He looks around for it in vain)* I'd better knock it in. *(He starts knocking it in with hammer to the consternation of the rest. He seems disturbed)* I do really need privacy for this operation!

(Ndem looks expectantly at Lieutenat who turns to Pastor)

Lieutenant:	Any chance, Pastor?
Pastor:	The holy barn is empty.
TWW:	*Barn? (Shrugs) Is it clean?*
Pastor:	Quite clean.
TWW:	Alright then. Let's go.

(He motions Ndem and Lieutenant to stay behind. Soldiers carry Mokai, and follow Pastor while TWW and assistant follow them towards exit. Ndem and Lieutenant look perplexed and confused)

TWW:	*(Stops at exit)* Major, what again is the full name of His Excellency?
Ndem:	General Finto Asantiko Baado.
TWW:	*(Repeats and writes in his notebook)* That'll be all.

(Lieutenant makes an impulsive move to follow the party. Ndem pulls him back)

Ndem:	Where to?
Lieutenant:	To keep an eye on things sir. *(Flustered)*
Ndem:	*(Looks after TWW)* A true genius. So lucky we have him.
Lieutenant:	*(Mechanically)* Yes sir. *(Confidentially)* But sir... he kept on about Russians.
Ndem:	Did he?

111

Lieutenant:	He praised Russians.
Ndem:	O' that! No, no. That was the apparatus. Russian made. *(Smiles patronisingly)* The gadget and not the maker. *(Confidentially)* Among other things, the Professor is the evil genius behind our foreign policy. *(Fore-finger on lips)*
Lieutenant:	Yes sir.
Ndem:	*(Quietly)* Now, this people here... and the General... the picture wasn't quite clear in your dispatch. He kept mentioning names and so on.
Lieuteant:	They all seem to adore him without knowing who he is... until now, that is. One of them, a girl, got shot by the RATS. The General must have been fond of her somewhat. *(Adds quietly)* She is Emily.
Ndem:	*(Nods reflectively)* I see.
Lieutenant:	I've made them swear in their chapel to forget whatever they know of him here. On the pain of death.
Ndem:	Good. And the Oath of Allegiance?
Lieutenant:	We are just working up to it sir. The Pastor has volunteered to form the Lord's Brigade to support the cause.
Ndem:	*(Intrigued)* Lord's Brigade?... *(Smiles approvingly)* Well that's an idea. Good. Very good.
Lieutenant:	Thank you sir.
Ndem:	Now that we have got the General, the menace of the Rats is all we have to face. Nothing definite is known about them except the naive name of Revolutionary Association of Tough Soldiers, and the silly slogan of 'Power to the People'.
Lieutenant:	They are no soldiers, sir...

Ndem:	We know... But they strike hard and move fast. We must stop them before they create further havoc. So be prepared for action.
Lieutenant:	Yes sir.
Ndem:	Rewards are for those who labour, eh?
Lieutenant:	Thank you sir. Sir... Permission to speak sir.
Ndem:	Yes.
Lieutenant:	*(Apprehensive)* I meant to ask sir... any news about Lt. Colonel Jeremiah sir?
Ndem:	*(Frowns)* The Rats got him...
Lieutenant:	*(Shocked)* They got him! *(Emotionally overcome, almost in tears)* Ah, Uncle J...!
Ndem:	C'mon, get hold of yourself, Soldier Boy.
Lieutenant:	He was my only mentor sir... The only one I ever had.
Ndem:	*(Comforting)* Now you have me. You have the entire Reformation Council.
Lieutenant:	Thank you sir... *(Hysterical outburst)* I'll get the Rats sir... I'll eat them alive... I'll...
Ndem:	Quiet! *(Listens intently to some noise far off)*
Lieutenant:	Yes Sir... sorry sir... *(Both listen with apprehension)*
Ndem:	What is that?
Lieutenant:	I don't know sir.
	(They listen some more. Lieutenant sends a soldier to have a look. Enter TWW very concerned)
Ndem:	*(Forestalls TWW)* How's he?
TWW:	He's responding tremendously. What's that? *(Meaning the noise)*
Ndem:	We'll soon find out. You better go back to him.
TWW:	Yes of course. *(Informing)* The Pastor has crossed over to his people.

113

Ndem:	*(Angry)* We forbade him!
TWW:	*(Going)* He's gone.
Ndem:	Disobedience!
Lieutenant:	I'll get him sir.
Ndem:	Flush them all out here at once.
Lieutenant:	Yes sir.

(He goes. He is shouting for Flock as he goes. Sentry comes back 'I See No-One Sir'. The sound moves nearer. Ndem is organising his men when Lieutenant comes back with Flock and Pastor)

Iya'jo:	*(Smiling mischievously)* It's them! I knew they'll come back, I knew it.
Ndem:	Who's them?
Pastor:	The heathens.
Ndem:	What heathens?
Iya'jo:	The cultmen. Akilagun on the war path.
Pastor:	*(Flexing muscles)* I'll handle them. The Lord did it once before: the Lord will do it again.
Flock:	*(Enthusiastic)* Halleluia!!!
Lieutenant:	Quiet!
Pastor:	*(Pleading)* Leave them to me, please General.
Ndem:	*(Angry)* I'm not general! *(To Lieutenant)* We can't take chances with all this nonsense. Take charge, Lieutenant.
Lieutenant:	Yes sir. *(He organises defence and ambush)* You... over there... you... over here. You go round the enemy. *(Turns to Pastor and Flock)* You and your people, just like the last time eh? But no singing this time. *(Gets his gun ready)*
Iya'jo:	*(Petrified)* Not again... please not again.
Lieutenant:	Shut up! *(To Pastor)* You are on oath.
Pastor:	*(To Iya'jo)* Yes. That's right. We're on oath.

114

(Pastor and his flock are left conspicuously on stage, while soldiers take positions not noticeable to a casual observer. The entire flock is struck with fear. Pastor stands still, arms folded looking like a statue.

Enter cultmen. They carry clubs, spears, cutlass and lasso rope. They are heavily laden with charms. All in various loin cloths with headdresses. A very young man — a boy, less adorned, is with them. He carries a cudgel. They chant in unison, but aggressive tone, doing a two steps forward and one step backward dance movement. Their rhythm increases as they come face to face with the Flock)

Lead:	*(Chants)* Oko'rò	It is poisonously bitter
Chorus:	*(Chants)* Agemo ò se é je!	The gecho's not eatable

(Repeat Lead and Chorus in rhythm and movements)

Lieutenant: Halt! Who goes there?

(Cultmen stop still)

Lieutenant: Drop your weapons and put your hands on your head.

(Cultmen look round not quite sure of the direction of the speaker. Pastor is full of nervous evil smile. Lieutenant repeats the order, no-one obeys)

I will count four. One... two... three...

(The young man charges forward with a battle cry. 'Ye Pah' waving his club in the air. He is shot dead on the run yelling and rolling to stillness. Terror strikes among the cultmen as soldiers emerge from their various positions covering the cultmen from all sides)

Drop your weapons, I say!

(Cultmen hesitatingly obey one by one, shocked beyond speech)

115

Iya'jo:	*(Hysterical)* They're killing off the youths!... Suffering of mothers!
Lieutenant:	Keep quiet!
Cult Leader:	*(Going to the fallen boy)* You killed our boy, stranger.
Ndem:	You disobeyed order.
Cult Leader:	We had no quarrel with you, stranger. You killed our little one...
Ndem:	Who are you?
Cult Leader:	*(Pointing to Pastor)* We are messengers on a mission.
Pastor:	They are the children of Satan from across the hills.
Ndem:	*(Exasperated)* What are you both saying?
Cult Leader:	*(Grief-stricken. Forgetting all else moves to pick up the dead cultman)* Ah! Kekere!
Ndem:	*(Feeling guilty)* He disobeyed orders.
Cult Leader:	What shall we tell his mother?
Iya'jo:	*(Shrieks)* The suffering of mothers!
Pastor:	*(Stopping Iya'jo, pulling her aside)* Sh!! Sh!!
Cult Leader:	*(Carries the body in his arms and looks at the faces of the guilty ones)* He's gone!
Ndem:	*(Motions to soldier to take the body from cult leader who hesitates)* Let him help you.
Cult Leader:	We have to take him back home.
Ndem:	You will. His parents will be duly compensated.
	(Cult Leader reluctantly gives boy to soldier, who takes it off stage)
Cultman:	*(Picks up dead one's club and carefully removes the elaborately adorned juju armlet from the club, and hands it over to cult leader)* He didn't wear it!

116

Cult Leader:	I thought so. The fool didn't wear it.
Ndem:	*(Curious)* What's that?
Cult Leader:	Ayeta.
Ndem:	Hm?
Lieutenant:	*(Scornfully interrupting)* His bullet-proof armlet.
Ndem:	I see. Pity about that. The Nation mourns truly and sincerely with you. I promise you, he shall be listed among the worthy casualties, whose blood has drenched the course of this epoch-making incident, in all our lives. *(Militarily)* That is that.

(Silence) |
Cult Leader:	*(Becoming aware of the Flock again)* But they hold our man.
Ndem:	What man?
Pastor:	*(On the mark)* What man indeed?
Cult Leader:	*(Accusing Pastor)* He knows.
Ndem:	*(Impatient)* What man are you people talking about?
Cult Leader:	The stranger that came and went in a strange way... leaving us without a High Priest. We know nothing of his past, but the Oracle will have no other successor but him, while he breathes the air of the Gods. It is him or perpetual autumn for us while he lives.

(Turns to the men for confirmation) |
Cultmen:	*(Together)* Yes.
Pastor:	Our side is different. They would want us to begin from the beginning, but I shan't...
Ndem:	*(Getting toughy)* Citizens. *(Silence)* Enough is enough. Whatever private squabbles between you will have to wait. Right now the entire Nation is in a state of emergency. And we here, you and I as loyal citizens, constitute the makers

117

of our Nation's destiny at this hour. *(Sternly)* Will you play your part or not?

Cult Leader: *(Lost)* What part?

Ndem: First , you will bury the hatchet with our friends here *(Indicating Flock)* in accordance with the policy of National Reconciliation right here and now. Right, Lieutenant?

Lieutenant: *(Clicks)* Right sir!

Ndem: I therefore order you both to step forward and shake hands as loyal citizens.

(Pastor eagerly comes out'to shake hands with reluctant and bewildered Cult Leader)

...And embrace!

(The two embrace awkwardly)

Ndem: Good. *(To Cult Leader)* Now what can you do for the Nation?

Cult Leader: *(Thoroughly bewildered)* Nation... What Nation?... We want to take our boy home for burial.

Ndem: You will do that. I take it you are all farmers?

Cult Leader: Yes. But the boy was a hunter, after his father.

Ndem: Hm! Right now, our friend here *(Indicating Pastor)* is organising the Lord's Brigade to serve the Nation. What do you think, eh?

Cult Leader: Think?

Ndem: Farmer's Brigade, eh?

(Leader is still lost)

I hand you over to the Lieutenant for the rest.

Lieutenant: Yes sir! *(To Cultmen)* Over here for the oath of allegiance.

Leader II: Where?

Ndem: Follow him

118

(They all exit rather apprehensively with Lieutenant in the direction of the Chapel. Pastor makes to follow them)

You stay.

Pastor: In our chapel!... please... taking heathens to swear on our altar!

(Ndem ignores him)

Charms and magic in Olifie!

Ndem: *(Irritated)* You have buried the hatchets, Pastor!

(Pastor shrugs)

You ought to be proud that your altar is in the service of the Nation as it were.

Pastor: Yes... *(Confidentially)* But they are of some secret cult.

Ndem: That too will be put in the service of the Nation.

Pastor: *(Thoroughly agitated and perplexed)* Yes... Yes...

Ndem: Calm down and don't let yourself down. The Lieutenant made a favourable recommendation of you. It is the first positive one to come from outside the forces since the crisis. I don't know what the Council will make of it, but eyes are on you.

Pastor: Eyes on me?

Ndem: What is your denomination?

Pastor: That of the Lord.

Ndem: C'mon man. *(He enumerates)* Cherubim and Seraphim, Celestial, Anglican, Apostolic, Methodist, Catholic... Baptist... You must have a name.

Pastor: *(Humbly)* We follow in the footsteps of the Lord himself. His church bore no name of fancy, except the place on which it was built — Olifie.

Ndem: You have to pick a name that will make you

119

	acceptable to the rest of the churches... in case... rewards are for those who labour. Understand?
Pastor:	*(In spite of himself)* Yes... Yes...
	(All sorts of noise comes from the direction of the Chapel. 'Halleluia' alternating with 'Eepah', obviously from Flock and Cultmen respectively. Pastor is alarmed)
	What's going on?... Shall I go and have a look?
Ndem:	*(Shaking his head)* No.
	(Enter TWW, beaming)
TWW:	Congratulations, Major.
Ndem:	*(Excited)* How's he?
TWW:	Couldn't be better... at this stage...
	(TWW whispers some details to Ndem, but Ndem is happily assured. TWW is going)
Ndem:	Shall I come?
TWW:	No, o... Just prepare to receive him. We have to try him on the people. Strictly under control.
	(Enter Lieutenant with Cultmen and the rest of the Flock)
	And remember... patience... lots of it at this delicate stage.
Ndem:	I understand.
	(Exit TWW)
Lieuteant:	Everything is alright sir.
Ndem:	Good. The General is coming.
	(Lieutenant organises the crowd for a reception)
Lieutenant:	You must all behave yourselves. And remember what we did.
	(Enter TWW followed by Mokai.)
	Mokai appears calm. He is dressed in the full uniform and epaulettes of a general. He is being ushered

120

	in by TWW, followed by TWW's assistants and guards. Ndem salutes)
TWW:	A remarkable recovery of a gallant soldier!
Ndem:	Wonderful, absolutely wonderful.
Pastor:	*(Shouting)* Glory be!
TWW:	Now, now, now, let's keep it under control, shall we? *(To Ndem)* We need some privacy, Major.
Ndem:	*(To Pastor)* Go join the Lieutenant and the others.
	(Pastor goes)
	Hearty congratulations sir!
Mokai:	Thank you. *(Pause)* I haven't heard any bird sing – for some time now.
TWW:	Birds. *(Smart)* The birds will sing in their time, sir. *(Joking)* The fact is, birds choose their time to sing, especially in autumn, your Excellency.
Mokai:	Autumn? Then it's harvest as well.
TWW:	That's right, your Excellency.
Mokai:	Autumn is harvest time, when all the leaves are flying away from the trees. Brown, yellow, green and the lot?
TWW:	O' yes. But seasons don't affect harvest any more. *(Pause)*
Mokai:	*(Shakes his head in mild protestation)* I am not a soldier. I am a servant of God.
TWW:	That's being everything, your Excellency.
Ndem:	*(Joins in obsequiously)* That's the whole point sir.
Mokai:	I said I am Mokai.
TWW:	'Was'. We did agree: no more anonymity.
Mokai:	*(Pause)* Alright, 'no more anonymity'. But too many sorrowful things have happened in the past.

121

TWW:	We know, sir, but the Nation wants you back.
Ndem:	The Nation needs you, sir.
Mokai:	I was condemned. I was chased and gagged ready for slaughter before the wind brought me here to Olifie.
TWW:	We can imagine, sir, very sorry about it, sir. They have paid dearly for their sins, sir.
Mokai:	I was on the run for a long time
Ndem:	All that's come to an end, sir.
Mokai:	*(Pause, as if reflecting)* You could be guilty before you were born.
	(TWW and Ndem are completely beaten)
TWW:	*(Guardedly homorous)* If you mean, visiting the sins of fathers on the children... I suppose you are right, sir.
Mokai:	The Old Wizard said that.
	(Iya'jo is startled)
TWW:	*(Without conviction)* Undoubtedly.
Mokai:	*(Shaking his head in wonderment)* All the way from the little cottage at the edge of the Savannah!
	(Iya'jo collapses on Pastor)
	...running ...flying ...hiding... with no place of my own...
TWW:	*(Taking control)* All that is now water under the bridge...
Mokai:	*(Interrupting)* ...Did you say water... did you say bridge... Under the bridge?
TWW:	No, your Excellency. I mean it is now all in the past. Now, the people want you back.
Ndem:	The Nation needs you, sir.
Mokai:	Really?
TWW:	It is a duty, sir. *(staring at Mokai)* You have to accept yourself, sir.

122

Mokai:	(With fixed gaze on TWW proclaims) Then, I am General Finto Asantiko Baado.
Ndem:	Without a doubt, sir!
	(TWW beams triumphantly)
Mokai:	(Suspiciously to Ndem) Who are you then?
Ndem:	(Caught unaware. Attention) Me? Sir, Major Daliki Nati Ndem late of the 39th Infantry Battalion of 3rd Commando Brigade.

(Mokai is looking through Ndem who fumbled a bit)

I was at Mons, sir. True, I've never actually had the honour of coming before your person, sir... I mean I've never had much access to the Supreme HQ; being in the far North with the 39th Brigade all the time, sir...

(Pastor and the rest troop in interrupting the proceedings. They take positions with Flock facing the Cultmen. Mokai stares round them all and back to Ndem)

Mokai:	(Starring) Yes?
Ndem:	(Continues, rather more relaxed) I have heard much about you sir, your exploit at the Academy, and all...
Mokai:	Fables, fables.
Ndem:	(Jocular) Not at all, sir. I have the good fortune of being through your Cadet House at Mons.

(Mokai manages a smile as he eyes Pastor, who is embarrassed)

The Commander, 'Mad Scot' Colonel Maclister MacBain always said I reminded him of you... sir... athletics, fatigue, target shooting, the army games up and down the Salisbury plains, sir... (Declaims smiling) Up Mons, up Artillery. Sir Major Daliki Nati Ndem of 39th Infantry

123

Battalion of 3rd Commando Brigade is your man, Sir. *(Salutes formally)*

(Mokai smiles. Lieutenant and all soldiers take cue and present arms, silence as Mokai pans round all faces present with TWW. Mokai declares:)

Mokai:	I am General Finto Asantiko Baado!
All Soldiers:	Long live the Nation! Long live Reformation! Long live General Finto, Asantiko Baado!

(Lieutenant prompts Flock and Cultmen to join in)

All:	Long live the Nation! Long live Reformation! Long live General Finto, Asantiko Baado!
Pastor:	*(Excitedly)* Halleluia...!
Flock:	Halleluia!
Leader:	*(Competing)* Yeah eh!
Cultmen:	Yeah Morisasegun! Hurrah, O' god of Magic!
Pastor:	Halleluia!
Flock:	Halleluia!
Leader:	Yeah eh!
Cultmen:	Yeah Morisasegun! Hurrah, O' god of Magic!
Pastor:	Halleluia!!!
Flock:	Halleluia!!!
Lieutenant:	*(Stops them)* That'll do... that'll do! .
TWW:	*(Goes to whisper in Mokai's ears)* You're doing well, sir. *(Signals to Ndem)* All yours, Major.
Ndem:	*(Opening his file)* Yes, the 'Run Down', sir.

(Ndem produces a paper which he glances at now

and again. Clears his throat and salutes very formally)

Here, at this hour, sir, in the presence of the Nations'Churches, and all other traditional forms of worship as represented here by the nucleus of the Lord's Brigade, the farmers of the Nation as represented by the nucleus of The Farmers Brigade; the team of patriotic civilian experts who have dedicated their lives to the cause of the Nation's rebirth as represented here by the one and only Professor O.T.K. Tomwuruwuru Ph.D., MD., M.T.K.D., L.T.S.P., who, among other things, is the renown Neurological Surgeon, Psychiatrist and Osteopath extraordinary; and lastly the armed forces, the Organiser, the executor and guide of the cause of the Nation as represented here by a detachment of Commando Reconnaissance Squadron under the command of Lieutenant Adibo Barbalu *(Lieutenant salutes proudly)*; the Supreme Military Council of the Reformation who held the Supreme Authority of the Nation in trust for your Excellency as represented here in the person of myself, Major Daliki Nati Ndem, I beg to celebrate your health with this brief account of the process that led to your ascendancy in the course of the last few tumultuous days in our National life, Sir! *(He salutes)*

(Hands over two typed sheets to TWW)

Please Prof... you will read the adjoin.

TWW:	Yes. Of course.
Ndem:	*(To TWW and Mokai)* It is supposed to be in chronological order but not quite. *(He reads on)* Major Buba and his platoon of·renegades...
TWW:	All dead, on account of being rubbed out by the ferret, in the Main Square while trying to resist lawful arrests.

125

Ndem:	Colonel Hatashia Binjojo...
TWW:	Dead. On account of being rubbed out with machine gun on his way to join the other conspirators with the keys of the armoury round his waist.
Ndem:	Colonel Olulade...
TWW:	Dead. On account of being rubbed out by a combination of rifle shots and grenade while trying to escape with haversack full of bank notes.
Ndem:	*(Becoming emotional)* Colonel Nwagwu, Col. Kaikara, Col. Olowojen, Col. Bintaka, and the decadent Major General Dende, Lt. Gen. Sofisa, General Shabakim, General Amedu Garuba and the entire Armour Training Unit, Officers of Bamboo, Bazuka Division; in the company of the notorious Field Marshall Jenju, the self appointed Redeemer, the corrupt gangster, and usurper of the people's Supreme Military power, and the wealth of the Nation, the traitor that sought to sell the Nation to the Russians, after his abortive negotiation with the Chinese, under the double dealing guise of National Socialism; while all the time he was buying Chateaux in Normandy, villas in Lausanne, mansions in London, Paris, Penzance and the far away islands of Puerto Rico, Montsarratt and oil city of Caracas.
TWW:	*(Who has been waiting patiently for his turn)* Dead. All dead, on account of being wiped clean off the face of the Earth and reduced to ashes by a combination of Boujeh grenades, mortars, napalm potatoes, and the fire that emanated from the four state petrol tankers, driven by four valiant patriots, who surrounded the so-called Supreme Headquarters, while the aforementioned vagabond gangsters were still planning further pillage of the Nation's treasury,

and a blood bath of innocent citizens to achieve their nefarious objectives...

(He seems bleary-eyed and in difficulty. Ndem discreetly takes over)

Ndem: The rest like Majors, Captains and their reactionary cronies who call themselves Revolutionaries are still being mopped up in pockets, in and around the capital. Final result sir, not a single officer above the rank of Major will cause your Excellency any further trouble; they are all dead.

Mokai: Dead?

Ndem: Dead as earth.

Mokai: You kill them all?

Ndem: *(Fumbles)* The loyalists lived up to their responsibilities, sir. Up Mons, up Artillery!

Cult Leader: *(Bored)* We want to go back to the village.

Lieutenant: Gotta wait for the Oath.

(Lieutenant moves smartly, tete-a-tete with Ndem. Ndem nods)

Ndem: *(To TWW)* The Oath.

Pastor: We are first.

Cult Leader: Never!

Lieutenant: Alright! You'll all have a go.

TWW: They'll have to be quick about it.

Ndem: They must. C'mon you of the Lord's Brigade.

(Pastor steadies himself, kneels and raises his staff towards Mokai)

Pastor: I, the simple servant of the Lord, in charge of the flock of the Meek Lambs of Olifie, do hereby, on behalf of the entire flock affirm publicly our allegiance to the...

(Lieutenant is prompting with his staff)

127

	... Reformation *(Prompt)* under the guidance of his Excellency, General Finto Asanitiko Baado
Flock:	*(Together)* Halleluia! Halleluia'! Halleluia!!!
Pastor:	*(Kisses his staff and rises)* Glory be! We have lived to see the day! It has often been said in the past! Can anything good come out of Olifie? Glory!
Flock:	Glory be!
Mokai:	You are the Pastor of Olifie!
	(Cult Leader recognises Mokai's voice. He peers at Mokai and exchanges glances with Cultmen understandingly)
Pastor:	Yes, your Excellency. Out of Olifie comes He that is greater than all of us. Behold the Apple of Olifie!
Flock:	Holy!
Cult Leader:	You claim nothing. There was Akilagun before Olifie.
Cultmen:	Yes.
	(Silence)
Iya'jo:	And before that?
	(Leader is lost for an answer)
TWW:	We can't have all this going on.
Lieutenant:	That's enough, citizens!
Iya'jo:	They asked for it. White pap dripped from black pot. There was a hill behind a hill; and another hill beyond it. White pap from black pots! There!
Cult Leader:	I thought you'd forgotten all that.
Ndem:	What's going on here?
Lieutenant:	Stop it all of you or else...
Cult Leader:	She is mother of earth. That's what.
Iya'jo:	You goof. You have eyes, but you cannot see. Mother of Earth indeed!

128

Flock:	Halleluia!
Cult Leader:	*(Defiant)* Ee Pah!
Cultmen:	Eee Paripah!
Leader:	*(Prostrating before Mokai and chanting)*

<table>
<tr><td></td><td>Idoo baa lee</td><td>It's in prostration</td></tr>
<tr><td></td><td>L'omo nki baba...</td><td>That sons greet father!</td></tr>
</table>

Cultmen:	*(Also prostrating)*

<table>
<tr><td></td><td>Idoo baa lee</td><td>It's in prostration</td></tr>
<tr><td></td><td>L'omo nki baba.</td><td>That sons greet father!</td></tr>
</table>

(Pastor is proudly aloof. TWW shakes his head helplessly in disgust as he looks at his watch)

Ndem:	Lieutenant!
Lieutenant:	Yes sir. *(Takes charge. Cocks gun)* No more nonsense of your private squabbles, you hear! Anymore of it, you have all your privileges withdrawn; Brigade or no Brigade. *(All is calm)* Good.
Pastor:	*(Meekly)* May I conclude, sirs?
Ndem:	Make it snappy. *(To Mokai)* Apology, your. Excellency.
Pastor:	I call on the precious little lambs of Olifie.

(Derin, Uzo and Titi come forward with small bowls with covers)

Open wide the petals of your roses;
Squeeze the honey down hard
To smoothen the glide of the Chosen One;
Along the thorny path of power,
And bedew his dry withering pine.

(Girls kneel at Mokai's feet to mime anointing his feet from their bowls. Mokai smiles discreetly)

To accommodate
His wisdom.

Girls:	Holy!

129

Pastor:	For his health.
Girls:	Holy!
Pastor:	The Nation.
Girls:	Holy!
Pastor:	And the glory of Olifie.
Girls:	Holy!
Pastor:	Forward the Reformation!
Ndem:	*(Spontaneously)* Bravo!
Soldiers:	*(Severally)* Bravo.
Pastor:	Father, Son, Holy Ghost!
Girls:	*(Simultaneously and overlaying)* Holy, Holy, Holy!!!
Derin:	*Wildly)* Super Jee!!
	(All stop)
Mokai:	Emily! Is that Emily?
Ndem:?	No, just a...?
Pastor:	No, just a little girl of Olifie.
	(TWW gestures frantically to stop it)
Lieutenant:	Alright,thank you... thank you... that'll be all...
Leader:	What about us?
TWW:	No, not again, Major.
Leader:	We don't mind if you don't want us. But our friend here, told us we had to do it.
Ndem:	Alright, just be brief.
Leader:	We do not have the gift of the circus.
Pastor:	What does he mean, the gift of the circus?
Lieutenant:	Take no notice. *(To Leader)* Come on, we haven't got all day.
	(Leader fumbles through his bag examining several elaborately adorned horns until he finds the right one. He opens it gingerly, and licks the

130

*contents with his tongue and steps forward
stretching the charm towards Mokai. He says a
short blood-curdling incantation in his native
language with intense concentration on Mokai.
His followers interpolate with ejaculation, 'Epo'!
'Epo'! i.e. oil to soften the impact of the
incantation and ward off adverse effect.
Everyone, even TWW, is momentarily
mesmerised. He ends with the following:)*

Leader:	To the ears of the Heavens To the ears of the Earth You are the Chosen One The nation chooses you, They gave you to us, Esa Cult accepts you.
Cultmen:	He eh pah!
Leader:	Akilagun accepts you.
Cultmen:	He eh pah!
Leader:	May your time bring peace in place of strife.
Cultmen:	Amin.
Leader:	May your time bring plenty.
Cultmen:	Amin.
Leader:	Right now, all we have is autumn, no harvest.
Mokai:	*(Interrupts)* No harvest?
Leader:	*(Desperately)* We want harvest in our time!
Cultmen:	We need harvest!
TWW:	*(Frustrated)* I think the Oath of Allegiance should be over, Major.
Mokai:	*(Louder)* Harvest?
Ndem:	The Oath of Allegiance is over, Lieutenant!
Lieutenant:	Yes sir. Everybody back to position.
Leader:	*(Backs up into his people, staring hard at Mokai)* We have no harvest.

Mokai:	You have no harvest. But someone said it's harvest all over.
TWW:	*(Obsequiously)* Perhaps they do not understand, your Excellency. Suppose I affirm it's harvest all over. *(To Cultmen)*
Cultmen:	We have none of it.
TWW:	You have none?
Leader:	None!
TWW:	Where were you when it all began to happen, my friend?
Leader:	Always been on our farms.
TWW:	Ah, farms! The wrong end of the stick. We speak of Harvest of nature.
Leader:	We laboured and laboured but no harvest for us.
TWW:	There is no need to labour, my friend.
Mokai:	No need to labour?
TWW:	No need your Excellency. In our situation it's nature labours and the Nation harvest.
Leader:	We do not understand all these in our village.
TWW:	Of course you don't.
Mokai:	*(Curiously as if thinking aloud)* Nature labours... and the Nation harvest!
TWW:	It's based on a well researched and tried principle of Advancement for Developing Nations of our calibre, your Excellency. For instance, there is always the timber, the manganese, the bauxite, the copper, the tiny-winny pieces of precious stones — all generously scattered around us by nature... and then the juice... oozing from the bottom of the deep to make us a power that can roar at will. (Smiles) Now, your Excellency, you can see how nature labours and all the nation need do is harvest in folds.
Leader:	We have had no share of it.

132

TWW:	Yóu will in due course; now that you are with us...
Leader:	Bunkum!
Ndem:	Language, Leader of Farmers Brigade, language!
	(Pause)
Mokai:	*(Breaking the pause)* Nature labours and the nation harvests. But the Lord said we must labour for the harvest, right, pastor.. Where is Pastor?
Pastor:	*(Very humbly)* Yes, your Excellency. Sweat for thy feed says the Lord. Halleluia!
Flock:	Halleluia.
	(Lieutenant raises his hand to stop Pastor)
Leader:	We must go now.
	(Mokai mutters inaudibly)
Ndem:	Your Excellency.
Mokai:	The Nation must labour! *(Authoritatively proclaimed)*
TWW:	The Nation must labour.
Mokai:	*(Simply)* Yes.
TWW:	We take it that it is a ruling from your Excellency?
Mokai:	Yes.
TWW:	Hear that, Major. 'The Nation must labour'. What a slogan!
Ndem:	A decree, Professor.
TWW:	Yes, of course. *(Jots points down in his notebook) Must go down in the speech to the Nation)*
Ndem:	*(Looks at watch)* Time Professor... the Capital is waiting.
TWW:	Yes... But can we really risk moving his Excellency right now?
Ndem:	Feeling better, sir?
Mokai:	I don't know.

(TWW signs to Ndem not to bother Mokai)

Leader:	What are we waiting for?
Lieutenant:	You will not interrupt again.
Ndem:	Danger of delay. The Nation stands still for every second we spend here, Professor.
TWW:	You are right; we have to make a move. But first things first, Major. The papers now, right?
Ndem:	Fast Professor

(TWW takes out an official agreement sheet, elaborately stamped and sealed. He moves close to Mokai. He offers Mokai a fountain pen with the papers. All with obsequious reverence)

TWW:	You have to sign this, sir.
Mokai:	What?
TWW:	*(Sweetly)* Papers, rather important documents that cannot wait, your Excellency.
Mokai:	Why?
TWW:	Why?... Why, your Excellency. Well, for a start the late regime have emptied the State Treasury. Clean. Maintenance of your Government will depend largely on these papers. *(Pause)* It is the fact of financing the treasury, your Excellency.

(Mokai seems umoved. Humbly)

Sign here, sir...

(Mokai looks at papers like some abstract painting then drops them)

Mokai:	I said why?
TWW:	*(On his tether. Obviously enraged and momentarily losing his head)* Why! Why!! Why!!! O' I could shoot myself. Why!

(Getting hold of himself, he picks up the papers)

Pardon me, your Excellency. You've taken on great responsibility. But it is good you know the

134

fact of it now... **For instance what do we do with our manganese, our tin... our copper... our oil... our precious stones and the rest? Even the timber? What do we do with them?** *(For effect)* **By ourselves?**

Mokai: *(Stubbornly)* **The Nation must labour!**

TWW: **Agreed... agreed, your Excellency. But before then...?** *(Desperately)* **You see if your Excellency will permit my immodesty, I did my second Ph.D thesis on 'The Pros and Cons of Economic Ties with South Africa'. It has since become the working papers for France, Germany, Jordan and a good bunch of British entrepreneurs, though they will never give due credits... So I do know what I am talking about.**

Mokai: *(Simply)* **Is that why?**

TWW: *(Exhausted but persists)* **There is much more to it than that, your Excellency. But I should not bother you with details at this point. As the Major had made clear, your boys are in firm control; but we still have ground to cover. For now, the Supreme Military Council of Reformation has entrusted me with diplomatic offensive.**

The Russians want to be friends: we are friends. But Obolensvky, their man in the capital is offering only some very vague technical assistance until we hear from Moscow. We have no time. The Chinese, friends of friends, enemies of friends, friends of enemies, enemies of enemies... a tight rope of diplomatic permutation you might say, your Excellency; the choice is theirs. The British have characteristically stayed neutral. That means they approve.

All other embassies are kept guessing under police surveillance except the French. I have got

135

the Council to understand that there should be nothing polite in dealing with the French. Ruthless opportunism. But then, we must bide our time... Priority! Be all that as it may, we still have to maintain our regime. In the meantime, we have secured America's *de facto* recognition on the assumption, on their part, that your Excellency's government will honour the 99 years bauxite, copper, manganese, petroleum and allied minerals agreement with the former regime. We keep them hoping until this paper *(Aloft)* is through. Your signature is what I am about, your Excellency.

Mokai: *(Simply)* Is that why?

TWW: Your signature on it means we are securing a hundred and twelve million American dollars ($112M) in credit on behalf of the nation. And that is only the tip of the iceberg. Right, Major?

Ndem: That's right.

TWW: See, your Excellency, 'the nation must labour'. But these papers will see the nation on its way. Money, your Excellency (Patronising joke) even our friends here of the Farmers Brigade will have no more autumns without harvest.

Leader: *(Brightens up)* You say we will have no more autumns without harvest?

TWW: With this *(Aloft)* you will have no more autumns without harvest. Come what may *(Pushing)* the nation must labour.

Leader: *(Mystified aloud)* The nation must labour.

Cultmen: *(In chorus)* The nation must labour.

TWW: That's it. The nation has begun to labour your Excellency. We have no time. Here. *(Puts papers close to Mokai to sign)*

Mokai: *(Pause)* You all want me to sign?

136

Leader / Pastor: (Severally) **Yes.**

(Mokai's shaking hand drops the pen. TWW gives it to him)

TWW: *(Decisively to Major)* This will reassure the Americans for now, eh Major?

(Major nods uncertainly. TWW watches closely as Mokai signs the document. He is triumphant)

That's it. Now you will witness here... *(Major countersigns)*

Ndem: *(Promptly)* Yes. *(He signs)*

TWW: Now it's all nice and legal. *(Puts papers away in his case)* Good. Now, we are ready for anything, Major.

Mokai: They really want me for Head of State.

Ndem: You are, already, sir.

Mokai: You hear that, Pastor...?

Pastor: Yes. It is the will of the Lord, your Excellency.

Mokai: Alright. Who and who will be my ministers?

Ndem: *(Thrown)* Ministers... well... it all depends on the choice from the loyal officers that make up the council down at the Capital. *(He looks at TWW who nods approval vigorously. He continues uncertainly)* But to start with here, sir... provisionally that is... I am to look after the bare essentials. State Security for one —

(TWW nods)

and that has combined with the Ministry of Defence, with or without Ministry of Works *(Fumbles)* ...being already earmarked for Chief of Staff Supreme Military Headquarters...

(TWW shakes head)

... all of this, of course subject to your Excellency's approval, sir...

137

Mokai:	You want to do all that?
Ndem:	If it pleases your Excellency to appoint me, the Lord shall be my strength.
Pastor:	Halleluia!
Flock:	Halleluia!
Ndem:	*(Takes cue sign from TWW)* But most important, Sir. It has been decided to recommend the candidature of our greatest civilian devotee, the same is Professor Tomwuruwuru to handle the Nation's Finance and Foreign Affairs plus all the intelligence network that goes with it... maybe Professor will like to enlighten his Excellency.
TWW:	No...not now, Major...
Mokai:	Not now. Birds do choose their time to sing, don't they?
TWW:	*(Humour)* Indeed, indeed your Excellency.
Ndem:	*(Impatient)* Do you certify that his Excellency can travel?
TWW:	I do *(To Mokai)* Feeling much better sir...
Mokai:	Yes.
Ndem:	Lieutenant. Get ready to move.
Lieutenant:	Ready everybody.
Leader:	Allow us to go to the village, to bury our boy.
Ndem:	Granted.
Iya'jo:	We want to come to the Capital
Pastor:	Yes, we are ready.
Ndem:	Not possible right now, Pastor. The government will send for... you and all of the Farmers Brigade at the appropriate time. But we have to say goodbye for now.
Mokai:	They cannot come with me?
Ndem:	Will be too heavy for security, your Excellency.

Leader:	We will be in the village.
Mokai:	I have to go alone, I suppose.
Pastor:	The Lord is not alone, your **Excellency**.
Iya'jo:	No loneliness with the Lord!
Mokai:	I am ready.
Ndem:	*(Announces)* His Excellency is ready!
All:	Long live the Nation! Long live Reformation! Long live General Finto Asantiko Baado!!
Leader:	*(To TWW)* You promise we will not have any more autumns without **harvest**!
TWW:	No. Never again!
Leader:	So be it!
Cultmen:	So be it!
	(As the party is about to move, Mokai is seated on a hammock to be carried by two soldiers - one in front and one behind)
Ndem:	*(Shakes hands with Pastor and Leader, and waves to the rest)* Goodbye... goodbye...
Iya'jo:	*(As if suddenly aware, declaims hysterically)*
	He's going! A time to meet, A time to part. Every parting like A piece of Death.
Pastor:	*Please don't talk of death, Iya'jo, please don't....*
Iya'jo:	Suffering of Mothers! I only talk of parting. You part to meet, You meet to part, Then you part, To meet no more...

(Iya'jo bursts into a chant as Mokai is being carried away with the entourage. Major and TWW waving. All except Cultmen – join Iya'jo, Pastor and Flock in singing:)

(Christian hymn)

A o paa de leti odo　　We shall meet
T'ese angeli tite e　　by the riverside
　　　　　　　　　　　　etc., etc.

(They exit DR. Cultmen exit UL. While the Flock stays put waving as they sing with Iya'jo being most vocal. The Cultmen chanting, carrying their dead, are going, but glancing back at the spectacle. Cultmen exit. The singing boils up. Flock is being possessed as Pastor and Iya'jo lead them on clapping with steps of all sorts. Suddenly, Derin becomes hysterical, shouting as she makes to follow the Mokai party)

Derin:　　Super Jee!
Take me along
Super Jee!

(She is held back. Iya'jo is petting her)

Let me go with Super Jee!
Super Jee!... Super Jee...

(From the direction of Mokai's exit comes the report of automatic gun fire and shouts of men fighting. The flock is struck still for a second, then breaks up as some of Mokai's party men run back in disorder. Only Iya'jo is left in far upstage, petrified still. Mokai is led in by a soldier)

Soldier:　　You're alright, Sir.

Mokai:　　*(Struggles with soldier)* Leave me alone... Go... before they get here. Go...

Soldier:　　I can't leave you, I can't...

Mokai:　　*(Struggles)* Go... I'm not your man... Go...

Soldier:　　*(Reluctantly scuttles off)* ... Goodbye, sir...

(Mokai is taking off his uniform as he crawls away in opposite direction while gunfire reports continue.

Slow fade out as gunfire subsides.

Light goes up slowly to reveal a huge cross standing on stage with a General's cap on it. Standing by it is Major Ndem, now Colonel, another officer in General's dress, and the soldier that helped Mokai in. Far away up left unnoticed by them is Iya'jo in mourning attire. Far away upright is Cult Leader, also unnoticed)

New General:	So this was the place.
Soldier:	Yes sir. The General fell right here. He ordered me to go on. I'm sure he willingly gave his life, sir.
Ndem:	No doubt. No doubt. But it doesn't seem we'll ever find his body now.
Soldier:	I'm ashamed I did not die with him. *(Hysterical)* I'm ashamed.
Ndem:	That's alright.
Soldier:	*(More hysterical)* I'm not fit to be in this uniform... I'm not
Ndem:	*(Shouts)* Pull yourself together!
New General:	No stigma. You are a good soldier.
Soldier:	Thank you, sir.

(New General salutes. So does Ndem and soldier. Iya'jo moves slowly towards them. They ignore her)

Iya'jo:	*(Quietly)* He was my son.
Ndem:	*(Gently sarcastic)* Oh was he?

(The Soldiers are going)

New General:	Who is she?
Ndem:	*(Derisively sarcastic)* The General was her son. *(Chuckles)* A pack of lunatics infest these woods. sir.

141

(They exit)

(Iya'jo goes slowly towards the vestry as light fades slowly on 'A o pade leti oodo...' off-stage)

Pause as cheerful chanting of cast of "Riwo, Riwo Yah"

Chorus: Riwo yea! yea! They all dance on waving to the audience as actors saying "Thank you and good night")

THE END